A New Owner's
GUIDE TO
AUSTRALIAN
CATTLE DOGS

JG-159

Overleaf: Australian Cattle Dog adult and puppy photographed by Isabelle Francais.

Opposite page: Ch. Barkersvale Supa Aussie owned by F. McKeown.

The Publisher wishes to thank the following owners of the dogs in this book: Michele Corwin, Yvonne and Frans DeJong, Arthur and Cheryl Edwards, T. Gardiner, Ann Gavett, Ralph and Susan Hannan, Sharon Jones, Ronald Lopez, B. Merchant, Suzanne Nevada, Margaret Price, Narelle Robertson, Grace Vance, Kim Wabel, Lyn Williams

Photographers: Ashbey Photography, Cabal Canine Candids, Arturo Chavez, Tara Darling, C. Edwards, Isabelle Francais, Ken Hammond, Karen Taylor

The author acknowledges the contribution of Judy Iby for the following chapters: Sport of Purebred Dogs, Health Care, Identification and Finding the Lost Dog, Traveling with Your Dog, and Behavior and Canine Communication.

© T.F.H. Publications, Inc.

Distributed in the UNITED STATES to the Pet Trade by T.F.H. Publications, Inc., 1 TFH Plaza, Neptune City, NJ 07753; on the Internet at www.tfh.com; in CANADA by Rolf C. Hagen Inc., 3225 Sartelon St., Montreal, Quebec H4R 1E8; Pet Trade by H & L Pet Supplies Inc., 27 Kingston Crescent, Kitchener, Ontario N2B 2T6; in ENGLAND by T.F.H. Publications, PO Box 74, Havant PO9 5TT; in AUSTRALIA AND THE SOUTH PACIFIC by T.F.H. (Australia), Pty. Ltd., Box 149, Brookvale 2100 N.S.W., Australia; in NEW ZEALAND by Brooklands Aquarium Ltd., 5 McGiven Drive, New Plymouth, RD1 New Zealand; in SOUTH AFRICA by Rolf C. Hagen S.A. (PTY.) LTD., P.O. Box 201199, Durban North 4016, South Africa; in JAPAN by T.F.H. Publications, Japan—Jiro Tsuda, 10-12-3 Ohjidai, Sakura, Chiba 285, Japan. Published by T.F.H. Publications, Inc.
MANUFACTURED IN THE
UNITED STATES OF AMERICA
BY T.F.H. PUBLICATIONS, INC.

A New Owner's
Guide to
Australian Cattle Dogs

Narelle Robertson

Contents

The Australian Cattle Dog is well known for his herding abilities.

The Australian Cattle Dog is athletic, intelligent, and hard-working.

The Australian Cattle Dog's loving and happy disposition makes him the ideal family pet.

Choose a puppy that is alert and active, with bright eyes and a shiny coat.

This lovely pair of Australian Cattle Dogs puppies pose for posterity.

HISTORY of the Australian Cattle Dog

The history of the Australian Cattle Dog is as varied as the history of Australia itself. The controversy that surrounds this history will always be subject to debate as there were few written records. Many years prior to European settlement on the vast island continent of Australia, there lived a wolf-like dog that was known to the Aboriginal population as "Warrigal," or Dingo. These dogs were primarily red in color, with few that were white or black and tan. They also carried a white tail tip and usually had white feet. These dogs were taken from their mothers even before they were able to see and were hand-raised by the Aborigines to produce a relatively tame dog that was taught to hunt and track.

The Australian Cattle Dog was developed to meet the needs of the 19th century rancher and became a legendary herder.

In the early 1800s, the first settlers, having limited availability of labor to control the large herds of cattle that grazed on unfenced properties and rugged bushland, set about to create a breed of dog to assist in mustering and moving wild cattle. The principal requirement of this breed of dog was that it was strong, possessed great stamina, and was able to bite. Initially, the cattlemen used bob-tailed dogs known as "Smithfields." They were big, rough-coated, square-bodied dogs, with flat, wedge-shaped heads, saddle flap ears, and bob tails.

They were black in color, with white markings around the neck that extended down the front. They were faithful, hardy, and sensible, but like all bob-tailed dogs, had an awkward cumbersome gait, were slow on their feet, and were unable to cope with the heat. They were also severe biters and barked too much. As the colony opened up and the herds increased, the need for a more active dog with less voice became pressing.

The ideal Australian Cattle Dog is as much a silent observer as he is a dog of action—alert to any stragglers and ready to return them to the fold.

In about 1830, a drover named Timmins from the Hawkesbury River area, approximately 60 miles north of Sydney, drove cattle down from Bathurst over the Blue Mountains to the Homebush Saleyards in Sydney. Timmins conceived the idea of crossing his dogs with the red native dog to produce the dog required, and thus originated the red bob tail, or "Timmins's Biters," as they were commonly called. Dogs of this cross were a great improvement on the Smithfields. They were very active and almost silent. Unfortunately, they possessed one very bad fault. If they were out of the drover's sight, they would chew the calf or cow nearly to pieces, demonstrating the Dingo instinct and influence. After a time, most of them died out, and the rough-haired Collie was tried next. Except in a small number of cases, they were also a failure, as they tried to work the cattle as if they were sheep, rushing to the head of the herd and barking. This action made the cattle wild, and was particularly bad for heavier cattle, as they would break and rush in all directions and therefore lose all their condition.

A cross of the rough Collie and Russian Poodle was tried next. Even today a few survivors of this cross may still be seen in old country towns–a blue, rusty, brown, or black dog with a coat like that of an Otterhound. They were very severe dogs, biting the cattle anywhere from head to tail, and their long coat made them particularly unsuitable for Australia's harsh summer conditions. Most soon died out. Crosses of the Bull Terrier and Collie were tried, but they proved to be too slow, too heavy, and too severe on the stock. In places where the cattle were very fierce, crosses of the Bull Terrier and Kangaroo Dog were also tried. They were very good for catching and throwing out outlaws, but useless for quiet cattle, so they died out too.

In 1840, a landowner by the name of Thomas Hall lived on "Dartmoor" at Muswellbrook, in the Hunter Valley of New South Wales, approximately 150 miles northwest of Sydney. He imported two smooth-haired blue merle Highland Collies (at that time called Welsh Heelers) from Scotland. Although these were considerably better than the common Collie, they proved to be less suitable for work with fractious cattle in the new, hostile, and unaccustomed environment, as they

The wild Dingo is just one of the breed's early ancestors crossed to produce the modern-day Australian Cattle Dog.

displayed some of the herding traits that were undesirable. Therefore, Hall experimented with native Dingo blood infusions, with the resulting litters becoming known as "Hall's Heelers." Just as the Dingo creeps silently from behind and bites, the pups followed this style of heeling, nipping at the fetlocks of the stragglers until they rejoined the herd. Immediately after the cattle dog nipped, it would flatten itself against the ground to avoid any kick a stubborn bovine might suddenly lash out. This dog was welcomed by grazier and drover alike for his ability to handle wild cattle, his stamina to travel great distances over all types of terrain, and his endurance in extremes of temperature. The physical appearance of the progeny closely resembled small, thickset Dingos, with their heads tending to be rather broad of skull, bluntly wedge shaped, with brown glinty eyes and pricked ears. Their color was either red or blue merle. Hall continued his experimental breeding until his death in 1870.

Word of Hall's new and superior Cattle Dog variety soon became widespread. Demand for the young stock spread rapidly throughout New South Wales, eventually reaching northern Queensland. Around this time, another landowner, George Elliot of Queensland, was experimenting with the crossing of the Dingo and Collie, producing some excellent workers. He entered into his diary on February 12, 1873, that his two-month-old quarter Dingo worked so silently on cattle, he called her "Munya," which is Aboriginal for silent.

In the early 1870s, these cattle dogs found their way to the Sydney markets and it was here that some breeders decided to refine these Hall's Heelers. A butcher named Fred Davis was the first to proudly display the ability of a pair of Hall's Heelers at the cattle sale yards in Sydney. Two brothers, Jack and Harry Bagust of Canterbury, in Sydney, were among several cattlemen to purchase pups from Davis. Mr. Robert Kaleski, a noted canine authority and respected journalist of the day, wrote, "Then a blue dog came on the field, called Bentley's dog, who was crossed through these dogs, and from whom all the latter day blue dogs of any note claim their descent. He was owned by a butcher working on Glebe Island, called Tom Bentley, and was a marvel for work and appearance.

Although his pedigree was never set out, we know beyond doubt that he was one of the pure Hall strain. From this dog on, selected

The Australian Cattle Dog at work is truly a marvel—tenacious, agile, and hardy.

Ligras Kim Orange Boy, "Jaffa," and Cranefield's Parakoola Dingo, "Matson," exhibit the distinct coat color that sets them apart from so many other breeds.

bitches, Messers Jack and Harry Bagust, C. Pettie, J. Brennan, A. Davis (Fred Davis's son who was my partner in the blue dogs for years) many other breeders, and myself made a start breeding the blue dogs. About 15 years ago we had them practically perfect."

The Dalmatian was introduced to improve the breed's rapport with horses, which was a fundamental requirement to satisfactory station and property work. The infusion of the Dalmatian changed the merle color to red or blue speckle. As with Dalmatians, the pups were born white, developing their color gradually from approximately three weeks of age. As much as the Dalmatian influence improved the dog's relationship with both horse and man, unfortunately some of the working ability was lost with this cross. The Bagust brothers, after admiring the working ability of the Black and Tan Kelpie, opted to introduce this cross with their speckled dogs. Thus they obtained a line of compact, highly intelligent, active, controllable workers, similar in type and construction to the Dingo, but chunkier of build with unique coloring and peculiar markings known to no other dog. The blue variety had black eye patches, black ears, and brown eyes, and all featured a small star in the center of the forehead region known as the "Bentley Star," due to the influence of Tom Bentley's dog. The body color was dark blue, often with black saddle and tan markings on the legs, chest, and head. The red variety displayed dark red markings in place of the black on an even speckled base.

In 1893, Mr. Robert Kaleski, the canine enthusiast and journalist, took particular interest in this new breed, and started showing them in 1897. His involvement proved to be of great assistance in fixing type and color, for he soon realized that there was no one to check on the judge and he could give the award in any way he fancied. In Kaleski's own words: "My partner and I showed a practically perfect Blue Cattle Dog by the name of Spot at one big show who was passed over for a lop-eared

One of the first Australian Cattle Dog champions, Robert Kaleski's Ch. Nugget, was a blue-speckled cross between a tame dog and a wild dingo.

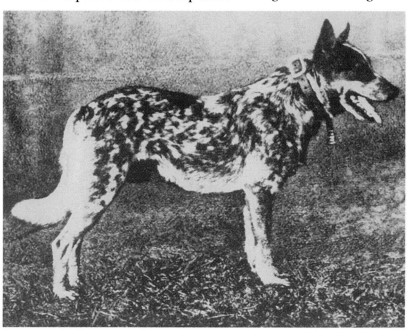

Today's Australian Cattle Dog not only excels on the range, but is one of the most popular breeds in Australia today. mongrel worth about five shillings. Alex showed Spot afterwards and was credited champion with him in a big class. I realized then that it was no use breeding good dogs true to type if this sort of thing went on, so I set to work to draw up a standard by which dogs could be judged and by which the judge was compelled to abide." Kaleski developed and stabilized the standard, and it was first endorsed by the Cattle and Sheepdog Club of Australia, then by the Kennel Club of New South Wales in 1903. He also drew up the standard for the Kelpie and Barb.

Kaleski's standard has been expanded over the years, but the essence of it is still very much a part of the official standard approved and adopted by the Australian National Kennel Council in 1963. Coincidentally, with the writing of Kaleski's standard, the breed's name officially became the Australian Cattle Dog, commonly known as the Blue Heeler, the Australian Heeler, or the Queensland Blue. From these unique beginnings the Australian Cattle Dog has developed into one of the most popular breeds in Australia today.

CHARACTERISTICS of the Australian Cattle Dog

The Australian Cattle Dog is one of the most versatile breed of dogs in existence today. Not only are they great working dogs, but they also make excellent family pets—they are loving, playful, and willing to please. They are courageous, tough, and intelligent, with strength and endurance unlike any other dogs of comparable size. They are very athletic, possessing the ability to work more than their fair share when required. Capable of quick and sudden movement, excelling both in wide-open spaces and in close quarters, Australian Cattle Dogs are renowned for their protectiveness and loyalty to master and property and are very selective of friends or foes. Although gentle by nature and curious but suspicious of strangers, they will show aggression if their master, family belongings, or property is threatened.

Australian Cattle Dogs are not naturally aggressive. However, they are very protective of anyone they consider their family or anything belonging to their family. Whether it is the house, the property, the family members, or the family car, this breed is ever alert and vigilant, and their presence is a usually sufficient deterrent to the most unwelcome visitor.

Because these dogs are excellent judges of character, strangers are very often treated to a thorough inspection—from

At only six months of age, Silver Hills Red Doll Anna tests her herding skills on a wandering lamb.

a distance if the dog is on unfamiliar ground, but more often at close quarters if in their own environment.

They bond very strongly with humans, but it is important to note that their master must dominate them, and the dogs must rigidly adhere to rules you set down for them. They are very loyal and that loyalty is usually proportional to their leader's dominance. They should know their place, and will get very frustrated when the rules are not clearly set. When on their home ground, they are exuberant, affectionate, extremely

The Australian Cattle Dog's loving and happy disposition makes him a welcome addition to most families. Joshua, Kaleb, and "Devon's Ziggy Blue" surely agree!

The versatile Australian Cattle Dog can become anything you want him to be! UCDX Mr. Here Comes Trouble CDX, TDX, BAD, CGC, QW, owned by Kim Wabel, is obviously very well accomplished.

playful, and strong willed. On occasion, life with an Australian Cattle Dog can be a frustrating battle of wits, especially when a puppy is pushing you to test your authority. Establishing yourself as the pack leader very early in the pup's life is vital because such an intelligent breed will take over as the "boss dog" if you allow it. This breed definitely has a mind of its own. They can quickly size up any situation, and if they are not made to understand who makes the rules, you will find yourself left out of any decision-making processes.

They must be kept occupied or they will occupy themselves by eating your new shoes or destroying your furniture. Although they make an ideal pet because of their gentle yet protective nature, their boundless energy and active minds are not suited for the elderly or the family that will leave the dog alone in the backyard for long periods of time.

The irresistible Cattle Dog makes a wonderful companion, but be certain to educate yourself about the responsibilities of owning a dog before you bring one, or a few, home.

As they tend to work silently, they are generally fairly quiet and will normally only bark when provoked in play or when alerting their master to an intruder. However, a dog that is bored will bark to tell his master that he requires attention.

It is important to understand the breed's temperament prior to taking an Australian Cattle Dog home; when given due consideration beforehand, this breed will give many, many years of dedicated companionship as well as total and unconditional love.

Two out of every ten person-dog relationships do not work out, although most could have. Often this is not due to physical problems such as disease or accidents, but unacceptable behavior on the part of the dog and the failure of the owner to train the dog properly. Most puppy owners will be confronted with at least some behavioral problems, so before becoming a statistic, make sure you understand the

In recent years the Australian Cattle Dog has become a formidable opponent in show rings around the world. The author, Narelle Robertson, puts Aust. Grand Ch.. Kombinalong Super Octane into his stance.

temperament of this breed. With a little preparation, they will give you all the companionship you will ever want or need.

THE VERSATILE AUSTRALIAN CATTLE DOG

Of all the continent's breeds, it is the Australian Cattle Dog that personifies the rugged outback of Australia. Tough, aloof, hard working, and extremely loyal, this breed is without doubt one of the most versatile in existence today.

The Show Dog

As a conformation show dog, the breed has in recent years become particularly competitive with many excellent specimens, gaining the ultimate Best in Show award on many occasions. The Australian Cattle Dog can been seen in show rings all over the world. There are many specimens being exhibited in the United States, Canada, Europe, South America, Japan, Asia, United Kingdom, New Caledonia; more recently their popularity as a show dog, working dog, and companion has reached South Africa, Kenya, India, and some of the more remote parts of the world.

The Obedience Dog

This is an area in which the Australian Cattle Dog excels. This breed has a natural affinity for obedience work. In general, herding breeds have generations of experience in following the master's hand signals when moving stock and are a far better bet at obedience work than perhaps a terrier that was bred to work on its own, killing rats in the farm shed.

The breed is very quick to learn and responds immediately to his master's signals and voice commands. They particularly enjoy agility, which is not only fun, but often has thrills and excitement for the handler, dog, and spectators alike. The best part of all is that the dogs love it.

Today Cattle Dogs generally work in parts of Australia where the scrub is still impenetrable by man. Ralph Hannan and "Doc" eagerly await their next adventure!

The Working Dog

The breed was initially bred to work, but with the introduction over the years of motor bikes and helicopters to herd the cattle long distances, the work of the Australian Cattle Dog, in most part, is confined to the yards. In some areas of Australia—where the dense scrub is still impenetrable to a man on horseback, and the modern stockman with their helicopters and motor bikes cannot get cattle out—the working Cattle Dog is sent in to bring out the beasts to the drovers. There is nothing more enjoyable than watching this breed doing what they were bred for. In most pups, the working instinct develops gradually, with the pup showing more and more interest in the stock. Unfortunately, this can be dangerous, as the pup can be subjected to being trodden upon or worse still, kicked by an aggressive cow or calf that the pup is annoying. It is therefore important that your pup is trained correctly if you wish him to work. This usually means working with an older, more experienced dog and handler. If you haven't had experience in training a dog to work cattle do not attempt to do so without guidance from an experienced stockman and trainer. The breed is naturally prone to work cattle, but they are not naturally able to herd without being trained.

The Australian Cattle Dog is perfectly at home as a devoted family member. These two pups enjoy a dip in the pool with their masters.

The Companion

There is no greater comfort than to spend time with man's best friend, and the Australian Cattle Dog is a totally devoted, loyal companion that only has eyes for one person—his master.

Any dog can make a good companion, and it is important to emphasize that your dog is totally dependent on you for not only your love and affection, but also for the physical requirements of feeding, housing, and general care. It is also in the development of the dog's character that your role is crucial, and it is here that you can produce a wonderful friend.

STANDARD for the Australian Cattle Dog

The Australian Cattle Dog has changed little since the late 1800s when the first standard was drawn up. In 1897, Robert Kaleski drew up the first Standard of Points for the Australian Cattle Dog, which was recognized by the original Kennel Club of New South Wales in 1903. This standard was not changed until 1963. Kaleski described the breed as a small thickset Dingo that has a head that is broad between the ears. This ensures that the dog has a large skull, hence plenty of intelligence. If the dog possesses a narrow skull, the brain must be small and the intelligence feeble, hence a poor worker. The head must taper to a point at the muzzle, meaning that the least weight is at the business end, ensuring that the dog can get his bite in quickly and then drop out of danger. This theory follows the same principle as the boxer using light gloves instead of heavy ones—his hitting is much quicker. He must be full under the eye, which ensures that the muscles that move the lower jaw are very strong. This is very necessary as they correspond to the biceps of a boxer and give the dog power to do his work. A

Aus. Am. Mex. Gua. Belize Int. Ch. Kombinalong Super Impact, winning his Mexican and International titles.

dog deficient there cannot continue biting long; his jaw muscles become tired. Strong and muscular jaws are vital. If there is a deficiency here, his jaw may be easily broken because there is no cushion of

LoneRun Rope 'n' Rustle demonstrates the strong, balanced, and compact appearance of the Australian Cattle Dog.

muscle to protect the bone and if injured, he is useless. The ears are short so that they can be readily laid flat when biting or fighting and are less likely to be damaged. They are pricked, so as to catch sounds such as whistles or words of command, especially from a distance. The ears run to a tip that is either V-shaped or diamond-shaped for two reasons. First, the progeny are more likely to be prick-eared, the ear muscles rising much higher in a diamond-ear than a "tulip" or spoon-shaped ear; second, the spoon-ear is a sure indication of the Bull-Terrier cross; set wide apart on the skull so that the ear inclines outwards rather than forwards. In the latter case, they do not hear so well; hence the dog cannot answer to the whistle or word of command as efficiently from a distance. The ears should be as pricked as a cat's for this reason.

The eyes are brown because that is the Dingo color, therefore considered the best. If blue or white, the animal is extremely likely to go blind or deaf, or both; in either case it will be useless for anything. They are quick because the dogs have to judge their distance every time when coming in to bite, and their eyes must be quick to do it. Sly-looking, because a hotheaded, rushing dog is useless as a worker, and the eye is the index to his character.

The shoulders are strong and well sloped so that the dog gallops easily and drops with ease when biting. Chest is deep because a shallow-chested dog has no heart room and is easily thrown off balance. If the chest is too deep, or "Bulldoggy" as Kaleski referred to it, he cannot travel at any speed, but it must not be out of proportion to the body.

Legs are clean, because a hairy-legged dog becomes weighted with mud on soft roads and soon tires. They should possess a fair amount of bone to carry a fairly heavy body. If he is too light in bone, he is top-heavy. Great muscular development is necessary, because without it he lacks the driving power to do the work; hence he is useless.

Feet are small and shaped like those of a cat, because this offers the smallest bearing surface for heat blisters on hot roads or thorns ("bindyi"). Also, when the foot is small, the power is more concentrated, giving better results. The shape of the Australian Cattle Dog's foot was a disputed point for some years. Some breeders argued that the dog with the splay or "hare" foot "sank less in soft ground," having a greater bearing surface. However, experience has proved that the cat foot is the best.

Back is straight, because a hollow-backed dog is always weak in the loins, and cannot drop or come back quickly enough when biting.

Ribs are well-sprung or "casky," which denotes a strong hardy constitution; "well-ribbed up" means that the last rib is close to the hip, thus enabling the dog to turn and twist his body easily. Good loins are important, for the reason that they are the hinge of the body, and if weak the body is useless. The loin should arch slightly because the dog's hindquarters are then of the Greyhound shape, giving him more speed and activity than a straight-backed dog. In my champion dog "Nugget," the arch is more pronounced; he was nearly as fast as a Greyhound, though very powerfully built.

Narelle Robertson and Aus. Ch. Kombinalong Super n'Salad exhibits the deliberate stance of the Australian Cattle Dog.

The hindquarters are strong and muscular because they are the "engine," or propelling power, of

Aust. Ch. Fijar Masked Bandit illustrates the sturdy compact condition that the Australian Cattle Dog is known for.

the dog. Some dogs are perfect in front but fail lamentably here; such dogs tire very quickly and do not earn their salt for a drover. Back thighs well let down for speed, because the lower the hock joints the longer the stride; hence more speed. No dewclaws are present on the feet, because they catch in the long grass or mud and tear the sinew, crippling the dog.

Tail is of fair length, for the reason that it regulates the dog's movements, being merely a continuation of the backbone covered with hair, and it serves to balance the dog in his gallop. If too short or too long, his speed and action suffer accordingly, just as with Greyhounds. The dogs are Dingo or bottle-shaped for two reasons: first, this shape of tail indicates Dingo strain, other than a long, thin tail denoting Bullterrier, or a short tail indicating the old Bob-tail. Second, a dog with a brush tail rests better then another, as in a wild state the dog sleeps coiled in a circle, with the nose buried in the fur of the brush. I don't know why exactly, but I believe that there is a physiological reason for it. Probably by lessening the respiration in this way, the dog conserves energy in the same idea as hibernation—otherwise suspended animation.

The coat must be short, smooth, and very dense, as the Cattle Dog have to work in all climates and all weather. Like the Dingo, the coat consists of two layers—a loose outer one to turn the sun's rays, and a short inner one, close and fine as a seal's fur, to keep out cold and wet.

A height of about 20 inches has been found by experience to be the best height for working purposes. They work well in all heights, but do not stand the constant work like the dog of 20 inches. Bitches, of course, should always be a little finer and smaller than the dog.

These two friends exhibit the acceptable coat colors of the Australian Cattle Dog: blue and red speckle.

Color is important for two reasons. First, that true blue color (neither light nor dark) is the most invisible color possible, particularly at night; hence a dog of this color is not easily seen by cattle or horses, and has the least chance of being kicked. Also, the markings and colors indicated in the standard represent purity of breeding. In every strain of blue Cattle Dog there is some peculiarity shown in the color as well as in the shape, so that an expert can tell by looking at any blue dog how he has been bred. Some breeds have objectionable traits in their strains (Bullterrier cross, etc.), and the color helps as a guide to pedigree. If the dog shows more black than specified, he is probably a Barb cross and hence timid and unreliable. If he is a whitey-blue, he shows Dalmatian cross and is very likely to be kicked or gored, especially at night as stock can watch him much better. He is also more liable to go blind and deaf.

Faults are specified so that the standard shall be rigidly adhered to and faults as described not allowed to creep in.

OFFICIAL STANDARD FOR THE AUSTRALIAN CATTLE DOG
   The following is the current standard of the Australian National Kennel Council 1994 FCI Standard Number 287 that was adopted by the AKC in 1998, with comments by the author in italics.

The General Appearance
   The general appearance is that of a strong compact, symmetrically built working dog with the ability and willingness to carry out his allotted task however arduous. Its combination of substance, power, balance and hard muscular condition must convey the impression of great agility, strength and endurance. Any tendency to grossness or weediness is a serious fault.
   The Cattle Dog must be viewed as a balanced, symmetrical dog with no part out of proportion to the whole. The breed is generic with every part of the dog balanced in moderation. Coarse or fine-boned specimens should be penalized.

Characteristics
   As the name implies, the dog's prime function, and one in which he has no peer, is the control and movement of cattle in both wide open and confined areas. Always alert, extremely intelligent, watchful, courageous, and trustworthy, with an implicit devotion to duty making it the ideal dog.
   The Cattle Dog above all else is a working dog and must be able to convey the ability to work. They should be happy, bright, intelligent, and always ready to defend master and property. A soft dog that is too fat and out of condition should be penalized heavily. They are athletes and must be kept in that condition.

Temperament
   The Cattle Dog's loyalty and protective instincts make it a self-appointed guardian to the stockman, his herd, and his property. Whilst naturally suspicious of strangers, must be amenable to handling, particularly in the Show ring. Any feature of temperament or structure foreign to a working dog must be regarded as a serious fault.

*A nervous, shy, or aggressive dog should be heavily
penalized.*

Head and Skull

The head is strong and must be in balance with other
proportions of the dog and in keeping with its general
conformation. The broad skull is slightly curved between the
ears, flattening to a slight but definite stop. The cheeks are
muscular, neither coarse nor prominent with the underjaw
strong, deep, and well developed. The foreface is broad and
well filled in under the eyes, tapering gradually to form a
medium-length, deep,
powerful muzzle with the
skull and muzzle on
parallel planes. The lips
are tight and clean. Nose
black.

*The Australian Cattle Dog's head
is strong and balanced, with
oval-shaped eyes and a broad
skull.*

*The head must be
balanced and wedged
shaped, with a broad
skull and muscular
cheeks. The skull and
muzzle must be on
parallel planes. The stop
is not 90 degrees but a
slight break between the
eyes. A guide to the
measurement of the head
is that from the point of
the nose through the eye
to the tip of the erect ear
across the skull back through the eye to the point of the nose
should measure a triangle. 1.5 to 1 ratio.*

Eyes

The eyes should be of oval shape and medium size, neither
prominent nor sunken and must express alertness and
intelligence. A warning or suspicious glint is characteristic
when approached by strangers. Eye color, dark brown.
*Far too often, one sees domed skulls with round
protruding eyes and muzzles that are too short. Round*

protruding eyes would be a hindrance to the dog while working, as the eye would collect dirt and foreign objects. Domed skulls are an obvious problem, as the dog would encounter a swift kick directly to the forehead rather than the kick going over the head.

Ears

The ears should be of moderate size, preferably small rather than large, broad at the base, muscular, pricked, and moderately pointed neither spoon nor bat eared. The ears are set wide apart on the skull, inclining outwards, sensitive in their use and pricked when alert, the leather should be thick in texture and the inside of the ear fairly well furnished with hair.

The standard calls for preferably smaller rather than larger ears. There is a tendency to have ears too big, incorrectly placed or of poor leather quality.

The Australian Cattle Dog has a pleasing expression—intelligent, happy, and alert.

Mouth

The teeth sound, strong, and evenly spaced, gripping with a scissors-bite, the lower incisors close behind and just touching the upper. As the dog is required to move difficult cattle by heeling or biting, teeth which are sound and strong are very important.

An older dog with worn teeth should not be heavily penalized, but any dog that did not have a correct scissors bite would indicate lack of strength as a biter. It is not a requirement of the breed to have 42 well-placed teeth and since the original breeds that make up the Australian Cattle Dog are commonly plagued with missing teeth, it would be difficult to expect full dentition.

Mi-De-B Sudden Stop "Travis," handled by Michelle O'Neill, exemplifies the Australian Cattle Dog's moderately sized, pricked, muscular ear carriage.

Neck

The neck is extremely strong, muscular, and of medium length broadening to blend into the body and free from throatiness.

Must be well muscled, clean, never throaty or carrying any looseness of skin.

Forequarters

The shoulders are strong, sloping, muscular, and well angulated to the upper arm and should not be too closely set at the point of the withers. The forelegs have strong, round bone, extending to the feet and should be straight and parallel when viewed from the front, but the pasterns should show flexibility with a slight angle to the forearm when viewed from the side. Although the shoulders are muscular and the bone is strong, loaded shoulders and heavy fronts will hamper correct movement and limit working ability.

The upper arm should join the shoulder blade as near to 90 degrees as possible. There is a great tendency to see a large number of short upper arms that do not allow for the correct extension required. Also, from the wither to the point of elbow should be equal to the point of elbow to the ground. This is a problem area where the chest extends past the point of elbow or the foreleg from the elbow to ground is too short. All these hinder correct, free, supple movement.

Body

The length of the body from the point of the breastbone, in a straight line to the buttocks, is greater than the height at the withers, as 10 is to 9. The topline is level, back strong with ribs well sprung and carried well back not barrel ribbed. The chest is deep, muscular, and moderately broad with the loins broad, strong and muscular and the flanks deep. The dog is strongly coupled.

Unfortunately, far too many dogs are too short in body (the dog should be 10 percent longer than high), which does not give the

Ch. Turrella Red Robin displays the clean-cut lines of the Australian Cattle Dog that are distinctive in this breed.

flexibility to turn quickly and thus restricts movement. Must be a well-ribbed back with a deep and powerful chest allowing for plenty of lung and heart room for maximum endurance. Deep, broad, and muscular loins with deep flanks are coupled together with balanced strong forequarters and powerful hindquarters.

Hindquarters

The hindquarters are broad, strong, and muscular. The croup is rather long and sloping, thighs long, broad, and well developed, the stifles well turned and the hocks

The Australian Cattle Dog has a deep, muscular, and moderately broad chest.

well let down. When viewed from behind, the hind legs, from the hock to the feet, are straight and placed parallel, neither close nor too wide apart.

The most common problem in the hindquarter would be the insufficient turn of stifle. The standard calls for well-turned stifle, but we do not want the angulation of a German Shepherd. Remember that the Australian Cattle Dog is moderate in every respect. We cannot therefore excuse the many straight stifles that are being exhibited today, which unfortunately leads to higher-than-required tail sets and lack of slope of the croup. This will cause lack of drive and stilted rear ends.

Feet

The feet should be round and the toes short, strong, well arched, and held close together. The pads are hard and deep, and the nails must be short and strong.

The attitude is, "No feet, no working dog."

Tail

The set on of tail is moderately low, following the contours of the sloping croup and of length to reach approximately to the hock. At rest it should hang in a very slight curve. During movement or excitement the tail may be raised, but under no circumstances should any part of the tail be carried past the vertical line drawn through the root. The tail should carry a good brush. *The tail should flow as part of the dog. It acts as a rudder for the dog in movement. All too often one sees a tail carried over the back like an antenna. This is normally caused by incorrect slope of croup and tail set too high. The tail should never hook or curl.*

Gait/Movement

The action is true, free, supple, and tireless and the movement of the shoulders and forelegs is in unison with the powerful thrust of the hindquarters. The capability of quick and sudden movement is essential. Soundness is of paramount importance and stilteness, loaded or slack shoulders, straight shoulder placement, weakness at elbows, pasterns, or feet, straight stifles, cow or bow hocks, must be regarded as serious faults. When trotting the feet tend to come closer together at ground level as speed increases, but when the dog comes to rest he should stand four square.

Correct movement is of paramount importance. Only a well-constructed dog is going to move correctly. Gait in itself is not soundness, but a measure of soundness and correct gait is not possible without correct structure.

Coat

The coat is smooth, a double coat with a short dense undercoat. The outer-coat is close, each hair straight, hard, and lying flat, so that it is rain-resisting. Under the body, to behind the legs, the coat is longer and forms near the thigh a mild form of breeching. On the head (including the inside of the ears) to the front of the legs and feet, the hair is short. Along the neck it is longer and thicker. A coat either too long or too short is a fault. As an average, the hairs on the body should be from 2.5 to 4 cm. (approx. 1-1.5 in.) in length.

The breed is required to work in all weather conditions; therefore, they must have adequate protection against the elements. The coat is a double coat with the outer coat approximately 1 to 1.5 inches in length and straight and the undercoat is softer and shorter to keep the dog warm in winter and cool in summer. Curly or wavy coats are sometimes evident in older dogs.

Color

Blue

The color should be blue, blue-mottled, or blue speckled, with or without other markings. The permissible markings are black, blue, or tan markings on the head, evenly distributed for preference. The forelegs tan midway up the legs and extending up the front to breast and throat, with tan on jaws; the hindquarters tan on inside of hindlegs, and the inside of thighs, showing down the front of the stifles and broadening out to the outside of the hindlegs from the hock to toes. Tan undercoat is permissible on the body providing it does not show through the blue outer coat. Black markings on the body are not desirable.

The coat of the Australian Cattle Dog is straight, flat, and tight on the outside with a short dense undercoat.

Red Speckle

The color should be of good even red speckle all over, including the undercoat, (neither white nor cream),

with or without darker red markings on the head. Even head markings are desirable. Red markings on the body are permissible but not desirable.

Although body patches are undesirable, an otherwise excellent specimen should not be penalized for a body patch. Unfortunately, the standard does allow for red and red mottle. The blues, however, have three variations of color with blue, blue speckle, and blue mottle.

Size

The height at the withers should be: Dogs—46 to 51cm (18-20 inches), Bitches—43 to 48cm (17-19 inches).

Dogs or bitches over or under these specified sizes should be penalized.

Faults

Any departure from the foregoing points should be considered a fault and the seriousness with which the fault should be regarded should be in exact proportion to its degree.

The Australian Cattle Dog should measure between 17 and 20 inches high at the withers.

Note—Male animals should have two apparently normal testicles fully descended into the scrotum.

Faults are common in all breeds of dogs and without them most of the challenge would go out of breeding. It is important, however, to be aware of the faults of your dog and try to overcome them. Faults are only an obstacle in our attempt to breed the perfect dog.

THE STUMPY TAIL CATTLE DOG

The Stumpy Tail Cattle Dog is the oldest of the recognized Australian breeds, with the exclusion of the Dingo. In 1830, a

The Stumpy Tail Cattle Dog is an entirely separate breed, not an Australian Cattle Dog with his tail cut off. Ch. Rokeglen Stumpy Shiraz owned by B. Merchant.

cattleman by the name of Timmins from the Bathurst area of New South Wales crossed the Smithfield, a black and white long–haired dog with a bobbed tail that drove from the Smithfield markets in England, with the native dog, the Dingo. The progeny were red bob-tailed dogs known as "Timmins's biters." These red bobtails were later mated with a blue merle, smooth-coated Collie. This produced both red bobtail dogs and blue or blue-mottled bobtail dogs; the latter having black patches on the head and some black patches on the body. By selective breeding of the bobtail to bobtail, the absence of tail became fixed in the breed. They were silent workers, though very severe heelers.

These dogs were the early ancestors of the Stumpy Tail Cattle Dog, which is an entirely separate breed and not just an Australian Cattle Dog with his tail cut off.

Although the Stumpy Tail is a relatively uncommon breed around the show ring, it is held in high esteem in country areas as a wiry, tireless, and intelligent worker.

The Stumpy Tail possesses a natural aptitude in work and control of cattle and is a loyal and courageous companion. Like the Australian Cattle Dog, he bites low and immediately crouches to evade the resulting kick.

At first glance, the Stumpy Tail Cattle Dog appears to resemble the Australian Cattle Dog, but closer scrutiny reveals that apart from the absence of the tail, there are several major differences.

The body is square and thus appears leggier. Also, there is a definite difference in color markings. Due to the absence of the black and tan Kelpie, which was used in the creation of the Australian Cattle Dog, the tan gene is absent; therefore, the Stumpy Tail does not possess any tan markings whatsoever. Their color is all blue or blue mottled. Body patches are quite allowable, even though they

Although at first glance he appears very similar to the Australian Cattle Dog, the Stumpy possesses several major defining characteristics.

Like the Australian Cattle Dog, the Stumpy Tail Cattle Dog possesses a natural ability to work and control cattle. are undesirable in the Australian Cattle Dog. The head is not as strong as the Australian Cattle Dog, tampering more to a wedge, and the nose color is black. Even though they possess strong bone, they are not as heavy in bone as the Australian Cattle Dog.

The temperament of the Stumpy Tail Cattle Dog is far more energetic than that of the Australian Cattle Dog. They possess an inexhaustible amount of energy and make excellent family pets. They are totally devoted to master and family. Whereas the Australian Cattle Dog will become aggressive if provoked, the Stumpy Tail Cattle Dog tends to step back and analyze the situation, asking for guidance from the master before dealing with the problem at hand. Unfortunately, they have a tendency to be a little nervous with strangers, partly due to the limited gene pool from which they are bred.

They are a rare breed in Australia, with only a handful of dedicated breeders working to improve and increase the numbers on that continent. They are currently a recognized breed only in Australia and New Zealand.

The following is the current standard of the Australian National Kennel Council, 1988:

The General Appearance

Shall be that of a well-proportioned working dog, rather square in profile with a hard bitten, rugged appearance and sufficient substance to convey the impression of the ability to endure long periods of arduous work under whatsoever conditions may prevail.

Characteristics

The "Stumpy" possesses a natural aptitude in the working and control of cattle, and a loyal, courageous and devoted disposition. It is ever alert, watchful and obedient, though suspicious of strangers. At all times it must be amenable to handling in the show ring.

Head and Skull

The skull is broad between the ears and flat, narrowing slightly to the eyes with a slight but definite stop. Cheeks are muscular without coarseness. The foreface is of moderate length, well filled up under the eye, the deep powerful jaws tapering to a blunt strong muzzle.

Nose black, irrespective of the color of the dog.

Eyes

The eyes should be oval in shape, of moderate size, neither full nor prominent, with alert and intelligent yet suspicious expression, and of dark brown color.

Ears

The ears are moderately small, pricked, and almost pointed. Set on high, yet well apart. Leather moderately thick. Inside the ear should be well furnished with hair.

Mouth

Teeth are strong, sound, and regularly spaced. The lower incisors close behind and just touching the upper. Not to be undershot or overshot.

Neck

The neck is of exceptional strength, sinuous, muscular and

of medium length, broadening to blend into the body, free from throatiness.

Forequarters
The shoulders are clean, muscular, and sloping, with elbows parallel to the body. The forelegs are well boned and muscular. Viewed from any angle they are perfectly straight.

Body
The length of the body from the point of the breastbone to the buttocks should be equal to the height of the withers. The back is level, broad and strong, with deep and muscular loins, the well-sprung ribs tapering to a deep, moderately broad chest.

Stumpy Tail Cattle Dogs are tremendously energetic and can make wonderful family pets when well trained. This group of Stumpys surely agrees!

Hindquarters
The hind-quarters are broad, powerful, and muscular, with well-developed thighs; stifles moderately turned. Hocks are strong, moderately let down with sufficient bend. When viewed from behind, the hind legs from hock to feet are straight and are placed neither close nor too wide apart.

Feet
The feet should be round, strong, deep in pads with well-arched toes, closely knit. Nails strong, short and of dark color.

Tail
The tail is undocked, of a natural length not exceeding 10 cm (4 inches). Set on high but not carried much above the level of the back.

Gait/Movement

Soundness is of paramount importance. The action is true, free, supple, and tireless, the movement of the shoulders and forelegs in unison with the powerful thrust of the hindquarters. Capability of quick and sudden movement is essential. Stiltedness, cow, or bow hocks, loaded or slackshoulders or straight shoulder placement, weakness at elbows, pasterns or feet must be regarded as serious faults.

Although the Stumpy Tail Cattle Dog is still a rare breed in Australia, dedicated breeders are working to improve the breed and increase their numbers on the continent.

Coat

The outer coat is moderately short, straight, dense and of medium harsh texture. The undercoat is short, dense and soft. The coat around the neck is longer, forming mild ruff. The hair on the head, legs and feet is short.

Color

Blue: The dog should be blue or blue mottled, whole colored. The head may have black markings. Black markings on the body are permissible.

Red Speckle: The color should be a good even red speckle all over, including the undercoat (not cream or white), with or without darker red markings on the head. Red patches on the body are permissible.

Size

Height: The height at the withers should be within the following measurements: Dogs—46-51cm (18-20 inches). Bitches—43-48 cm (17-19 inches). Dogs or bitches over or under these specified sizes are undesirable.

Faults

Any departure from the foregoing points should be considered a fault and the seriousness with which the fault should be regarded should be in exact proportion to its degree.

Note: Male animals should have two apparently normal testicles fully descended into the scrotum.

SELECTING the Right Australian Cattle Dog for You

Most people embark upon the purchase of their first puppy with some hesitation. Few newcomers to a breed know what to look for as far as breed type, including the finer points and conformation. Hopefully, the cautious buyer will not rely too much on his own judgement, especially if he contemplates showing his pup. However, some people imagine that they have an "eye" for a dog, and if this is the case, it would seem worthwhile to go ahead with a personal choice. The gamble may well pay off, more by sheer luck than good management. However, to pick a show winner from a litter of bouncing, jumping, biting, eight-week-old Australian Cattle Dog puppies is a very chancy endeavor, and even many people with years of experience in the breed would hesitate to pronounce too categorically what a puppy will look like when he matures.

To make sure of getting at least the best pup available, it is wise to deal with a reputable breeder. This does not necessarily mean the biggest names or largest kennels. The breeder you want is one who breeds good dogs, exhibits them often, and wins consistently at shows under many different judges. They should have been breeding for quite a number of

Be sure to do your homework and learn all you can about the breed before making the decision to bring an Australian Cattle Dog into your home.

years, by which time you will find that they have established a good bloodline. Their stock should be recognizable at once by its hallmark of quality and type.

When good breeders produce Australian Cattle Dogs one year, they will look like those they bred the year before and the year before that, and when you visit their kennel you should find that the breeding

At eight weeks of age, Roshara's Mountain Mica, owned by Ann Gavett, takes a break to smell the flowers!

and showing stock all look alike. This is the kennel you should be able to trust to supply you with a good quality puppy. Tell them what you want, explain your

Australian Cattle Dogs are social creatures and need attention and play time when young. Andrew and Philip Price seem to be the favorite playmates of these six-week-old pups.

ambitions in the breed—whether you want a show dog, a working dog, or a pup for companionship. You will no doubt get good and fair treatment, with a very good chance of coming away with what you want. Such a breeder knows their stock intimately and will find it reasonably easy to select the best dog for your purposes.

Make up your mind before you start that you will take plenty of time to make your selection. Go armed with a copy of the standard, having studied the contents in detail before arriving at the breeder. The dog or bitch you buy will probably be your companion for the next 14 years or more, so choose carefully. Get first impressions; these have reasonable importance and almost certainly will at once dismiss a few of the puppies put before you.

Like mother, like daughter! Often the temperament of a puppy will be much like her parents.

It is important to put color preference in the background. Dog flesh comes first, color second. Although you may love the look of a blue dog, it would be a mistake to bypass a superior specimen because he was red.

Always try to make your own pick from the litter. If you have only two to choose from, it is probable that the best ones have already been sold. Let the puppies run free in their pen and later around your feet if at all possible. Maybe, as the five or six puppies bound around you, you will note one that is particularly appealing to you. In effect, do not buy the dog you do not take to at first sight. View with caution the puppy that slinks away into the rear of the kennel or shies away from your outstretched hand. Natural wariness of strangers is fine, but in excess these can be the symptoms of unreliability, a characteristic not common and definitely not wanted in this breed.

If available, view the parents, especially the mother. She must have a good temperament. The mother's influence on a puppy's temperament is enormous. This is partly because the pup inherits her disposition, but mainly it is her behavior and

This little guy looks about ready to make his escape! Playfulness and activity are often signs of a healthy and well-adjusted puppy.

attitude as a mother that molds the pup's personality. A nervous, timid mother is likely to raise fearful pups that are much less liable to develop into suitable companions or show or working dogs.

Ask the breeder to let the litter run free, preferably on the grass. Then the puppies will gallop and play, revealing their basic limb movements to the full. Some of the puppies will dash off at once on their own adventures, but a few friendly and curious ones will besiege you. These can be lifted one after the other and examined. Try to find a waist-high table or kennel on which to place each puppy carefully, reassuring the uncertain ones.

There is no telling what life has in store for the Australian Cattle Dog puppy you choose—he may be a champion or companion—but he'll definitely be your best friend!

The Australian Cattle Dog pup is born white and will change color to either red or blue within a few weeks of birth. In most cases, the color of an eight-week-old pup will be lighter than the color that the dog will be eventually. Also, at this age the ears will be dropped. This is quite normal and they will become erect at any age up to six or seven months.

To commence your detailed examination, first check that the puppy has no discharge from the eyes and that they are bright and clear. Check that the color of the mouth is a healthy pink and that the jaws and teeth are correctly placed. The ears should be clean and the puppy well covered, but not fat. Run your hand down the puppy from head to tail making sure you check the tail for any kinks or lumps. The Australian Cattle Dog's coat should be thick, although in a two-month-old puppy it will seem more open than one worn by an adult, and this must be taken into consideration. Avoid the puppy with a dull, dry coat, or one that is standing up. He may be "wormy," and like his coat, the eyes will inevitably be found to be dull as well.

Turn the puppy over on to his back; examine the belly, groin, and armpits. Question the breeder about any spots or rawness you may find there. Sometimes young puppies coming off the kennel floor or dampened by the licking of their kennel mates look a little red below, but such soreness soon disappears once they are on their own. Look at the genitals, too—a male dog should be complete, i.e., with both testicles descended into the scrotum. A cryptorchid (with neither testicle down) or a monorchid (with only one testicle descended) is useless to you if you wish to breed later. It is not always possible, however, to see two testicles in a small puppy, although it should not be difficult to feel them, and it is important to find out at this point. Keep an eye open for any discharge evident from the penis (or vulva in the case of a female puppy). Lift the tail and examine the anal region to ensure a healthy condition. The puppy's navel should be looked at in case a slight rupture has occurred. Umbilical hernias, unless big, need not perturb you, although it is better to buy a puppy without one. The veterinarian can deal with them quite simply when the puppy is a month or two older.

Your Australian Cattle Dog will have a good start in life if his parents are happy and well adjusted. Try to see the dam and sire of the puppy you are considering.

Most people can assess the condition of the puppies presented to them, and the breeder owes it to you to present his stock for purchase in good coat and health. Once you have completed your examination of the puppy and are completely satisfied with your choice, the breeder will detail to you what the puppy has been fed and what vaccinations the puppy has received. He should give you a health certificate, diet sheet, vaccination certificate, pedigree papers, and all necessary paperwork for you to take home with your new family member.

CARING for Your Australian Cattle Dog

Adding a new pup to your family can be one of life's most rewarding acts, and the health and happiness of your new addition is something that will always be of paramount importance. Just as people are learning that they are at risk of certain health problems due to their environment, lifestyle, and heredity, our pets are also vulnerable to risks: poor breeding, inadequate housing, improper diet, insufficient health care, and too little exercise, to name but a few of the hazards that will shorten and diminish the quality of their lives.

Your Australian Cattle Dog's crate should be made into a cozy den where he can relax. Kuma, owned by Ronald Lopez of Hawaii, seems perfectly at ease.

Puppyhood is a time when your new dog will experience rapid behavioral, physical, and physiological changes. From 3 to 12 weeks of age, a puppy begins to assume adult characteristics and to learn to respond to his environment. It is the first time a puppy is capable of learning, and it is a perfect time to work on housetraining and simple obedience commands.

HOUSETRAINING

If you intend to allow your new pup in the house, then logically you will want him to be housetrained. A pup cannot be fully housetrained until he is about four months of age, but you can certainly start the moment you bring your new pup home by showing him what is expected. Although this is the most difficult way

Your Australian Cattle Dog will look to you, his owner, to take care of his needs.

to housetrain a pup, many people choose to paper train them first and wait until they are older to train to go outside.

Choose a small space, preferably one that can be closed off, and cover the floor in newspapers. Initially, this is where the pup will spend most of his time, so try to make it as comfortable as possible. Place the pup's bed in one corner and make sure that the newspaper covers all of the floor space.

Praise the pup when he eliminates on the paper, but make sure that you always take him outside after a meal, after play, and after waking up from his nap. Praise him when he eliminates outside and encourage him to do so as much as possible. It will not take long for the pup to understand that if he eliminates either on the paper or outside, he will get praise and sometimes a special treat. Remember, though, that it is difficult to train a pup to wait until you take him outside, as a young pup's immature bladder simply cannot take the wait of four or five hours in between walks. It is equally important to note that you must not punish your pup when he messes in the wrong place. If you see your pup start to go in the wrong spot, quickly pick him up and put him on the paper or outside. Then praise him as usual for going where he is supposed to go. If you are too far away to reach your pup, do not rush over and scare the pup by swooping on him. Instead, try to call him to distract his attention from the matter at hand. Don't forget to praise your pup when he stops and take him outside immediately to finish his business.

BASIC TRAINING

Taking care of your new family member is hard to do when you are tired and have no time. Take care of yourself physically and emotionally first. If the dog is taking care of you, guess who is in charge? Observe your relationship with your Australian Cattle Dog and notice

The time you invest in training your Australian Cattle Dog will benefit the both of you for a lifetime. Good training will enable both of you to live life to its fullest.

Very basic training can begin at a relatively early age, once a puppy has been vaccinated and housebroken. when you are rewarding your dog for his behavior, especially if you do not like the behavior he is displaying during training. Australian Cattle Dogs tend to be dominant because they are very intelligent, clever, brave, and resourceful, which means they are good at getting their way. They are also watching you and working out their relationship with you. Long before their brains have matured and they have control of their actions, they are struggling to be "pack leader." Be smarter than your dog. You must act like a leader. Being the alpha in the relationship does not always mean acting out the alpha role. It means that you are the leader, the most fun, in control, and the smartest. Make your dog earn privileges. Keep some favorite toys that only you control access to. He should learn to behave in order to get rewards such as snacks, petting, playing, and snuggling. He should perform the sit, down, or stand command to get attention. Putting your puppy on his back and gently holding him there until he submits to a belly rub is a good way to establish yourself as leader.

Your new pup will have energy to burn and your aim is to channel this energy into acceptable activities, therefore minimizing destructive behavior such as digging holes, pulling the washing off the line, and chewing up your good shoes and furniture.

There are simple ways to show your dog that you are in charge that will make training sessions fun rather than a battle. You can play games with your Australian Cattle Dog that make training fun for this intelligent, creative, and easily bored dog. When he is in another room, call your dog. If he comes, shower him with lots of fun rewards. Give your dog treats. Throw the ball, play fetch, or do whatever excites your dog. If your dog does not come to you, then show him you had something really great and then completely ignore him. Your dog will understand that he missed out. Games build the foundation for training and reinforce to the dog that paying attention to you is important.

Do not call your dog to punish him (this gives him an unintentional negative association). Do not call your dog to do something he hates, like nail clipping. Yes, you have the right to clip his nails, bathe him, or do anything else that needs to be

A young puppy will not know the difference between good and bad behavior. It is up to you, the owner, to teach him what is acceptable in your household.

done. Just call him for something else and then, while he is there, clip his nails. Never chase your dog, yelling, "Come." Teach "come" when you are in control of your dog. You will teach your dog that you are the smartest, fastest, and strongest by the way you play games. Make sure you win and that the games are played with you in control, not your dog.

Positive rewards like praise, petting, and small rewards of food are far more effective than punishing misdeeds. Patience, praise, and persistence are the key words in gaining a balanced obedient companion. It is much better for your dog to associate good deeds with reward than for him to fear pain and discomfort if he makes a mistake. However, verbal punishment is necessary. The message must be clear and delivered immediately, while your dog is in the act of the misdeed. After that period of time, your dog will not know what he is being punished for.

Although they look harmless, the Australian Cattle Dog will need discipline and guidance to become a valued family member.

Once you are consistent with your message of good behavior to your dog it will not be necessary to reward him every time he does what you want. Intermittent reward is far more effective than always or never being rewarded.

Remember that if you are really too busy to train your dog, you probably shouldn't get one at all. Owning a dog is a real commitment for people, and the proper training is necessary to produce a well-mannered and cherished companion.

EXERCISE

Australian Cattle Dogs are not lap dogs or lounge lizards and they will need a large area in which to exercise when you are not spending time with them. It is important to play with or walk your new pup for at least 30 to 60 minutes a day to avoid obesity and to interact with your puppy, familiarizing him to his environment and human companions. Remember, though, do not overdo it in the early stages of your pup's development. His bones are soft and easily damaged. As your pup matures, the bones will harden, but in the meantime you must be careful. Avoid long runs and hard uphill work. Walk your pup on a lead and maybe take him to the local park so that he can interact with other dogs. Lead training is often ignored but is vitally important, particularly with today's strict dog laws. If you live in an urban area, teach your pup to enjoy walks and he will never miss the running free that only his country cousins are permitted. If your pup initially balks on the lead, bend over, pat your knee, and call him to you with whatever command you normally use. Lean down and pat the ground to attract attention. Praise him when he comes to you; never punish him when he doesn't. If necessary, give the lead a sharp jerk, purely to startle your pup into action. Immediately let the lead go loose and praise again for the quick response. Even if you only

Although Australian Cattle Dog puppies are known for their energetic and playful nature, this little guy knows that getting his beauty sleep is important too!

Even though Australian Cattle Dogs are not generally considered good cooks–this little guy seems to think that a pot is the perfect place for a nap! manage to walk one step, never drag your pup along by the neck. Coax your pup rather than force him. No matter how long it takes, be patient–it will pay off in the end.

DIET

Throughout your Australian Cattle Dog's lifetime, he should be fed a nutritionally balanced diet specifically formulated for his age and lifestyle. Feeding pups poor quality, inexpensive food can not only slow down their growth rate, but can also cause poor muscle and bone development and will decrease their resistance to infectious diseases. Giving your puppy the right food need not be a difficult or complicated task, and the correct diet will reward you with a healthy dog.

A high-quality dog food that provides the proper nutrition and is fed in appropriate quantities is crucial to your Australian Cattle dog's development. You should be aware that too much food or too much of certain nutrients can actually be quite dangerous. Overfeeding can cause obesity or accelerated growth and it can cause a predisposition to malformation of

Puppies grow very quickly and require especially nutritious meals to grow into healthy adults.

the joints, increasing the possibility of hip dysplasia, crooked limbs, and inflamed joints. Too much dietary calcium during a puppy's growth period may also contribute to skeletal abnormalities and lameness.

Make sure you have all the necessary food required for your puppy as outlined in the diet sheet provided by your breeder. If the breeder did not provide you with one, your veterinarian can help you pick the right food for your dog. Follow the instructions carefully. Any abrupt changes in the normal feeding schedule, brand of food, or amount given can cause stomach upset and diarrhea. If you wish to change your Australian Cattle Dog's food, do so gradually by mixing a small amount of the new brand with the old, slowly increasing the ratio until you have changed the diet completely. A puppy diet should be fed to your Australian Cattle Dog up to the age of one year, and then replaced with an adult diet. If you are unsure about any feeding concerns, do not hesitate to contact your breeder or call your veterinarian.

HOUSING

Prior to bringing your new puppy home, it is important that a suitable exercise area is provided for your new family member. Keep in mind that your new puppy will probably spend a considerable amount of time outdoors, therefore a dog run and a shelter from the elements are required. The amount of room you provide for your new dog depends on how much backyard or land you have. If you plan to give your dog the whole backyard, make sure that there are no escape routes, for he will find them very quickly and will be off exploring the neighborhood in no time. It is advisable that even with a yard, you should build a run with a kennel attached to put the dog in when required.

It is important to provide your Australian Cattle Dog with cool fresh water at all times.

With this is mind, make sure that the run is constructed on dry, well-drained ground. Concrete is generally satisfactory as it can be easily and quickly washed down with a hose. The dog's area can be made of several different materials, but keep in mind that it is preferable to have a waterproof surface not only for protection from the elements, but for easy cleaning. Make sure that the kennel is facing away from the afternoon sun so the dog may be able to retire to a shady spot. No dog will thrive unprotected in the scorching sun any more than he will in the bitter winter weather. The kennel roof and sides should be insulated from the wet. Inside the kennel, make the dog comfortable and most importantly, make sure your dog is dry. If the surroundings are damp it will affect your dog's health.

Your new puppy will initially be overwhelmed by his new surroundings and will become easily stressed about being away from the others in the litter. Your puppy will need to spend plenty of time with his new family. Set up a special area of your house that he can play in, and be sure to give him plenty of attention. The Australian Cattle Dog loves to be with people and will make a wonderful house dog if you acclimate him to the rules of your family.

TO BREED OR NOT TO BREED?

You are now the proud owner of a pedigreed Australian Cattle Dog, and like any other proud owner of this unique and wonderful breed, you will now contemplate whether or not you want to increase your family unit by breeding your dog. Obviously, if you have purchased a male then you must go and purchase a female to be able to breed. If, however, you have purchased a female, then all you need do is establish whether your bitch is good enough to be bred.

A breeder's aim is to produce an animal that is at least as good as the one he or she owns, or better, if possible. If you are able to achieve the latter, then you will have done a worthwhile service to the breed and will feel a real sense of achievement. Unfortunately, few breeders possess what can be claimed as a sound working knowledge of genetics. Many dog owners claim to have an "eye" for a dog and this instinct has held many in good stead in their time and enabled them to produce, by good assessment of the dog and bitch, some worthwhile stock. If, however, she is an average specimen with her fair share of faults, then your task is perhaps more difficult. At least you have the right to try to improve upon her by careful selection of the male. An average bitch that is true to type is good enough to breed, but always keep in mind that breeding an average bitch to an average dog will only produce average pups, so select your male dog very carefully in an endeavor to improve the quality of the litter.

If you are one of the lucky owners who bought a quality bitch and have picked the right dog for her, you stand a fairly good chance of successfully breeding. However, only the people that have the time and the resources to care for the mother and all the pups produced should consider breeding their dogs. Good homes must be found for every puppy born, and the mother's and pup's health must be carefully monitored. Vaccinations are needed for the litter and trips to the veterinarian are necessary. If all of this seems daunting and you have decided that you do not have the time to devote to this endeavor, have your dog or bitch altered prior to their first season. It will help to protect your Australian Cattle Dog from certain diseases as well as help to control the pet overpopulation problem that exists throughout the world.

CONGENITAL PROBLEMS

Like most breeds, the Australian Cattle Dog has hereditary and congenital problems that the new owner should be aware of and they should discuss these problems with the breeder prior to the purchase.

Progressive Retinal Atrophy (PRA)

This is a degenerative disease of the retinal cells that progresses to blindness. The disease is commonly known as "night blindness" and is a hereditary condition that is

Breeding dogs of only the best quality ensures that good health and temperament are passed down to each new generation.

recessively inherited in all breeds studied to date.
Unfortunately, the problem is widespread in Australian Cattle
Dogs. It is a gradual deterioration of the retina, the area at the
back of the eye where images are turned into electrical signals
to be sent to the brain. The nervous elements of the retina
undergo progressive atrophy and
the dog suffers from impaired
vision. To attempt to correct this,
the pupil dilates widely, even in
daylight, and the dog's
expression becomes staring. At
night or at dawn or dusk, the dog
is unable to avoid objects and
runs into them, but during full
daylight he appears to see quite

*Since many diseases
known to the Australian
Cattle Dog are inherited, it
is important to purchase
your pup from sound
breeding stock that has
been fully examined for
congenital problems.*

well. The dog will slowly go blind and there is no cure. The
condition is further complicated by the mature age onset of the
problem, most commonly between four and eight years of age.
There are cases reported in Australia, the United States, and
Europe. It is a recessive autosomal gene and both parents need
to carry the gene for it to show up in the offspring. If only one
parent is carrying the gene, some of the pups will eventually
show symptoms of PRA, some will carry the gene, and others
will be clear. Currently, the only method of detecting PRA is
through a clinical examination by a qualified veterinarian/
ophthalmologist. No treatment can arrest the progressive
degeneration and the dog gradually becomes blind.
Responsible breeders are aware of the condition and have their
breeding stock tested. Affected dogs should not be used for
breeding and responsible breeders will only breed from those
dogs tested clear.

Luxating Patella

There are many types and degrees of patella luxation. The
patella or kneecap can luxate or dislocate medially, toward the
body midline, or laterally, away from the midline, and can be
traumatic or congenital in origin. The problem has been
evident in Australian Cattle Dogs for some time, and the breed
suffers from lateral luxation in most cases diagnosed. Surgical
correction is not usually necessary unless the dog shows
symptoms such as pain or gait abnormalities. Your veterinarian

can easily diagnose the condition and a simple check of the patella can be performed by your veterinarian to see if the dog is predisposed to the condition. Dogs that are showing signs of the problem should not be bred, as studies show that in about 50 percent of cases treated surgically the dog demonstrates reoccurring patellar luxation in as short a time as one year. Affected stock will pass on the problem to their offspring.

Deafness

To date, studies of congenital deafness in the dog are limited, although those breeds with the highest prevalence include the Australian Cattle Dog, Australian Shepherd, Bull Terrier, Catahoula, Dalmatian, English Cocker Spaniel, English Setter, and West Highland White Terrier.

Inherited congenital sensorineural deafness is usually, but not always, associated with pigmentation genes responsible for white in the coat. Because the Dalmatian is influential in the overall makeup of the Australian Cattle Dog, the breed is unfortunately plagued with this problem.

These playful pups know that an umbrella can keep them dry—it is also the perfect toy for some fun and games!

Purchasing an Australian Cattle Dog from a reputable breeder will ensure that your dog has a long and healthy life. Amanda and James Hannan share hugs and kisses with Ch. Kombinalong Too Super.

Through extensive research it has been established that deafness does not develop in dogs until the first few weeks of life, with normal development occurring to that point. Studies have shown that Australian Cattle Dogs do not go deaf until three to four weeks after birth. The histologic pattern that occurs in most dog breeds is known as cochleo-saccular or Scheibe-type of end organ degeneration.

Since the ear canal does not open until approximately 14 days of age in dogs, and deaf puppies cue off the responses of littermates, it is not uncommon for deafness to go unrecognized for many weeks. In some breeds, deaf puppies will display more aggressive play with littermates because they do not hear cries of pain, but after weaning deaf puppies will not waken at feeding times unless physically shaken.

Assessment of the presence of auditory function requires a simple test known as auditory evoked response or BAER. In this test, a computer-based system detects electrical activity in the cochlea and auditory pathways in the brain in much the same way that an antenna detects radio or TV signals.

Management of deafness comes back to the old saying, "You must be cruel to be kind." A bilateral or fully deaf pup is better off being euthanized, as the quality of life for deaf dogs is greatly diminished. Unilateral deafness, which means the dog has full hearing in one ear only, is an easier problem to manage and these dogs make ideal pets. The owners are often unable to detect any impairment. Some dogs with unilateral deafness will show a directional deficit and may not be immediately reactive to your presence if sleeping soundly with the good ear on the ground. However, there is no evidence to euthanize unilaterally deaf dogs, although they should not be bred. Breeding fully hearing dogs will eventually, with the cooperation of all breeders, prevent further affected dogs and the ultimate increase in the prevalence of the disorder.

Hip Dysplasia (HD)

This appears in many breeds of dog. In some breeds it is the most common cause of osteoarthritis or degenerative joint disease. The term "dysplasia" is a developmental condition that results in abnormal looseness or laxity of the hip joints.

The signs of HD vary from decreased exercise tolerance to severe crippling, although some dogs may never shows signs of dysplasia and generally remain very fit and active. Even though a large percentage of Australian Cattle Dogs today do not work stock, they channel their energy and intelligence into other activities, including obedience, agility, tracking, showing, and being the active family member. Exercise diminishes the effects of this common and often crippling disease.

When searching for an Australian Cattle Dog puppy, do as much research as possible and avoid making a hasty decision.

Any diagnosis of hip dysplasia must be made via expert radiographic diagnosis. This involves taking X-rays of the joint and typically sending the film to organizations that will evaluate, register, and certify the dog. You cannot make a reliable diagnosis of HD on the basis of external symptoms such as lameness or gait. All dogs should be certified free of this disease before being bred.

Playfulness and activity are often signs of a healthy and well-adjusted puppy.

Upon selection of your Australian Cattle Dog puppy, the breeder should offer a guarantee against inherited disorders.

GROOMING Your Australian Cattle Dog

Keeping your dog's coat in good order requires only a few minutes of thorough brushing each day. Your dog will love the attention. As you brush through the coat with a good quality pin brush, be sure to watch for any signs of rashes, wounds, open sores, parasites, etc. Your Cattle Dog will molt usually twice a year, once in spring and then again in autumn. They possess a thick double coat, and it is important when the coat is shedding to remove all the dead undercoat and any mats that have developed around the hindquarters, tail, and the heavy ruff around the neck. It is quite natural for you to brush what seems like buckets of hair out of your dog during this period and this twice-a-day grooming routine will alleviate the problem of dog hair everywhere. The friction of

Turrella Blue Devilwoman obviously enjoys showing off her good grooming for the camera. Remember, a well-groomed dog is a happy dog, and a happy dog is a healthy dog!

the brush will help to stimulate the skin and tone the muscles, disposing of dead hair and activating the growth of new. A poorly groomed coat is also a haven for external parasites, and proper grooming will help you control fleas and ticks.

BATHING

Normally, it is unnecessary to bathe a Cattle Dog much more than occasionally unless you are pre-show bathing to bring him into competition brilliance. Puppies, however, seem to sometimes roll in noxious matter and will need an urgent bath, but generally speaking, bathing a young dog is an exercise best left until after all puppy vaccinations are completed.

Never bathe a dog immediately following a meal. If possible, avoid very cold days if the dog has to go outdoors after the bath. Dogs are best bathed indoors and the whole operation should be conducted with the minimum of fuss. No dog should have unhappy memories of his first bath. He should be

encouraged to enjoy the proceedings and the sense of well-being he gets from the final rubdown with the towel. It is a good idea to place a rubber mat on the floor of the bath so your dog does not slip.

There are many excellent dog shampoos available, some that assist with flea control. Follow the instructions and after the final rinse, towel down well, particularly under the body and around the genital area. If the weather permits, a brisk walk would be in order to allow your dog to shake any excess water, and then back inside to complete the towel down and finish with a brush through the coat.

DENTAL CARE

Good dental habits established early can ensure that your dog will be free of any dental disease and the buildup of plaque and tartar. Dogs do not tend to suffer from cavity problems like humans, but they do

POPpups™ are healthy treats for your Australian Cattle Dog. When bone-hard they help to control plaque build-up; when microwaved they become a rich cracker that your Aussie will love. The POPpup™ is available in liver and other flavors and is fortified with calcium.

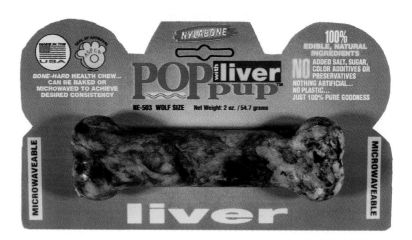

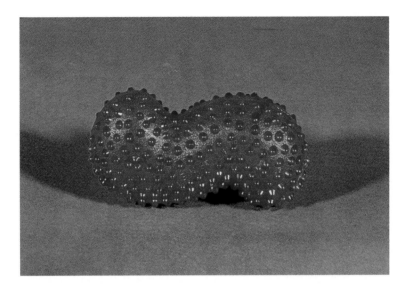

The Hercules™ is made of very tough polyurethane. It is designed for Australian Cattle Dogs, who like to chew. The raised dental tips massage the gums and remove the plaque they encounter during chewing. develop a variety of gum problems if their teeth are neglected. It is an excellent idea to begin gently opening your pup's mouth to examine the teeth, gums, and tongue on a regular basis. Not only will you detect potential problems early, your pup will be unafraid of your veterinarian's oral examinations later.

Dogs have two sets of teeth. The temporary teeth will start to emerge by the time the pup is three weeks of age and will continue to emerge up until six weeks of age. These teeth usually start to fall out from about four months of age when the permanent teeth erupt. Teething normally does not bother the pup. There may be the odd occasion where the pup is reluctant to eat and drools a little, but this tends to only last a few days.

It is advisable once the permanent teeth are through to begin gently brushing your Australian Cattle Dog's teeth with a soft toothbrush and water. If done regularly this will ensure that his teeth will last as long as they possibly can. Also chew toys like Nylabones® will ensure that the teeth are kept in pearly white condition and will help eliminate bad breath.

SPORT of Purebred Dogs

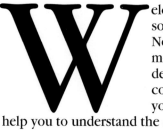

Welcome to the exciting and sometimes frustrating sport of dogs. No doubt you are trying to learn more about dogs or you wouldn't be deep into this book. This section covers the basics that may entice you, further your knowledge and help you to understand the dog world.

Dog showing has been a very popular sport for a long time and has been taken quite seriously by some. Others only enjoy it as a hobby.

The Kennel Club in England was formed in 1859, the American Kennel Club was established in 1884 and the Canadian Kennel Club was formed in 1888. The purpose of these clubs was to register purebred dogs and maintain their Stud Books. In the beginning, the concept of registering dogs was not readily accepted. More than 36 million dogs have been enrolled in the AKC Stud Book since its inception in 1888. Presently the kennel clubs not only register dogs but adopt and enforce rules and regulations governing dog shows, obedience trials and field trials. Over the years they have fostered and encouraged interest in the health and welfare of the purebred dog. They routinely donate funds to veterinary research for study on genetic disorders.

There are so many activities that your dog can participate in and the versatile Australian Cattle Dog has the ability to excel at them all.

Below are the addresses of the kennel clubs in the United States, Great Britain and Canada.

Shown as part of the Herding Group at AKC-sanctioned shows, many Australian Cattle Dogs enjoy successful careers in the show ring.

The American Kennel Club
51 Madison Avenue
New York, NY 10010
(Their registry is located at: 5580 Centerview Drive, STE 200, Raleigh, NC 27606-3390)

The Kennel Club
1 Clarges Street
Piccadilly, London, WIY 8AB, England

The Canadian Kennel Club
111 Eglinton Avenue
East Toronto, Ontario M6S 4V7
Canada

Today there are numerous activities that are enjoyable for both the dog and the handler. Some of the activities include conformation showing, obedience competition, tracking,

agility, the Canine Good Citizen Certificate, and a wide range of instinct tests that vary from breed to breed. Where you start depends upon your goals which early on may not be readily apparent.

Puppy Kindergarten

Every puppy will benefit from this class. PKT is the foundation for all future dog activities from conformation to "couch potatoes." Pet owners should make an effort to attend even if they never expect to show their dog. The class is designed for puppies about three months of age with graduation at approximately five months of age. All the puppies will be in the same age group and, even though some may be a little unruly, there should not be any real problem. This class will teach the puppy some beginning obedience. As in all obedience classes the owner learns how to train his own dog. The PKT class gives the puppy the opportunity to interact with other puppies in the same age group and exposes him to strangers, which is very important. Some dogs grow up with behavior problems, one of them being fear of strangers. As you can see, there can be much to gain from this class.

Puppy kindergarten is a wonderful way to introduce your Australian Cattle Dog pup to early training and basic commands.

There are some basic obedience exercises that every dog should learn. Some of these can be started with puppy kindergarten.

Sit

One way of teaching the sit is to have your dog on your left side with the leash in your right hand, close to the collar. Pull up on the leash and at the same time reach around his hindlegs with your left hand and tuck them in.

After winning a puppy class in the Clarence District Kennel Club show, Fijar Masked Outlaw is certain that life has great things in store for him!

As you are doing this say, "Beau, sit." Always use the dog's name when you give an active command. Some owners like to use a treat holding it over the dog's head. The dog will need to sit to get the treat. Encourage the dog to hold the sit for a few seconds, which will eventually be the beginning of the Sit/Stay. Depending on how cooperative he is, you can rub him under the chin or stroke his back. It is a good time to establish eye contact.

Down

Sit the dog on your left side and kneel down beside him with the leash in your right hand. Reach over him with your left hand and grasp his left foreleg. With your right hand, take his right foreleg and pull his legs forward while you say, "Beau, down." If he tries to get up, lean on his shoulder to encourage him to stay down. It will relax your dog if you stroke his back while he is down. Try to encourage him to stay down for a few seconds as preparation for the Down/Stay.

Heel

The definition of heeling is the dog walking under control at your left heel. Your puppy will learn controlled walking in the puppy kindergarten class, which will eventually lead to heeling. The command is "Beau, heel," and you start off briskly with your left foot. Your leash is in your right hand and your left hand is holding it about half way down. Your left hand should be able to control the leash and there should be a little slack in it. You want him to walk with you with your leg somewhere between his nose and his shoulder. You need to encourage him to stay with you, not forging (in front of you) or lagging behind you. It is best to keep him on a fairly short lead. Do not allow the lead to become tight. It is far better to give him a little jerk when necessary and remind him to heel. When you come to a halt, be prepared physically to make him sit. It takes practice to become coordinated. There are excellent books on training that you may wish to purchase. Your instructor should be able to recommend one for you.

Recall

This quite possibly is the most important exercise you will ever teach. It should be a pleasant

Oftentimes a treat is all the incentive an Australian Cattle Dog will need to behave!

Handlers must wear comfortable, practical clothing that does not distract attention from the dog they are showing. experience. The puppy may learn to do random recalls while being attached to a long line such as a clothes line. Later the exercise will start with the dog sitting and staying until called. The command is "Beau, come." Let your command be happy. You want your dog to come willingly and faithfully. The recall could save his life if he sneaks out the door. In practicing the recall, let him jump on you or touch you before you reach for him. If he is shy, then kneel down to his level. Reaching for the insecure dog could frighten him, and he may not be willing to come again in the future. Lots of praise and a treat would be in order whenever you do a recall. Under no circumstances should you ever correct your dog when he has come to you. Later in formal obedience your dog will be required to sit in front of you after recalling and then go to heel position.

CONFORMATION

Conformation showing is our oldest dog show sport. This type of showing is based on the dog's appearance—that is his

Successful showing requires dedication and preparation, but most of all, it should be an enjoyable experience for handlers and dogs alike. structure, movement and attitude. When considering this type of showing, you need to be aware of your breed's standard and be able to evaluate your dog compared to that standard. The breeder of your puppy or other experienced breeders would be good sources for such an evaluation. Puppies can go through lots of changes over a period of time. Many puppies start out as promising hopefuls and then after maturing may be disappointing as show candidates. Even so this should not deter them from being excellent pets.

Usually conformation training classes are offered by the local kennel or obedience clubs. These are excellent places for training puppies. The puppy should be able to walk on a lead before entering such a class. Proper ring procedure and technique for posing (stacking) the dog will be demonstrated as well as gaiting the dog. Usually certain patterns are used in the ring such as the triangle or the "L." Conformation class, like the PKT class, will give your youngster the opportunity to socialize with different breeds of dogs and humans too.

It takes some time to learn the routine of conformation showing. Usually one starts at the puppy matches that may be AKC Sanctioned or Fun Matches. These matches are generally for puppies from two or three months to a year old, and there may be classes for the adult over the age of 12 months. Similar to point shows, the classes are divided by sex and after completion of the classes in that breed or variety, the class winners compete for Best of Breed or Variety. The winner goes on to compete in the Group and the Group winners compete for Best in Match. No championship points are awarded for match wins.

To the victor goes the spoils! Ch. Kombinalong Supreme poses proudly with his many trophies.

A few matches can be great training for puppies even though there is no intention to go on showing. Matches enable the puppy to meet new people and be handled by a stranger–the judge. It is also a change of environment, which broadens the horizon for both dog and handler. Matches and other dog activities boost the confidence of the handler and especially the younger handlers.

Earning an AKC championship is built on a point system, which is different from Great Britain. To become an AKC Champion of Record the dog must earn 15 points. The number of points earned each time depends upon the number of dogs in competition. The number of points available at each show depends upon the breed, its sex and the location of the show. The United States is divided into ten AKC zones. Each zone has its own set of points. The purpose of the zones is to try to equalize the points available from breed to breed and area to area.The AKC adjusts the point scale annually.

The number of points that can be won at a show are between one and five. Three-, four- and five-point wins are considered majors. Not only does the dog need 15 points won under three different judges, but those points must include two majors under two different judges. Canada also works on a point system but majors are not required.

Dogs always show before bitches. The classes available to those seeking points are: Puppy (which may be divided into 6 to 9 months and 9 to 12 months); 12 to 18 months; Novice; Bred-by-Exhibitor; American-bred; and Open. The class winners of the same sex of each breed or variety compete against each other for Winners Dog and Winners Bitch. A Reserve Winners Dog and Reserve Winners Bitch are also awarded but do not carry any points unless the Winners win is disallowed by AKC. The Winners Dog and Bitch compete with the specials (those dogs that have attained championship) for Best of Breed or Variety, Best of Winners and Best of Opposite Sex. It is possible to pick up an extra point or even a major if the points are higher for the defeated winner than those of Best of Winners. The latter would get the higher total from the defeated winner.

At an all-breed show, each Best of Breed or Variety winner will go on to his respective Group and then the Group winners will compete against each other for Best in Show. There are seven Groups: Sporting, Hounds, Working, Terriers, Toys, Non-Sporting and Herding. Obviously there are no Groups at speciality shows (those shows that have only one breed or a show such as the American Spaniel Club's Flushing Spaniel Show, which is for all flushing spaniel breeds).

Earning a championship in England is somewhat different since they do not have a point system. Challenge Certificates are awarded if the judge feels the dog is deserving regardless of the number of dogs in competition. A dog must earn three Challenge Certificates under three different judges, with at least one of these Certificates being won after the age of 12 months. Competition is very strong and entries may be higher than they are in the U.S. The Kennel Club's Challenge Certificates are only available at Championship Shows.

In England, The Kennel Club regulations require that certain dogs, Border Collies and Gundog breeds, qualify in a working capacity (i.e., obedience or field trials) before becoming a full

Champion. If they do not qualify in the working aspect, then they are designated a Show Champion, which is equivalent to the AKC's Champion of Record. A Gundog may be granted the title of Field Trial Champion (FT Ch.) if it passes all the tests in the field but would also have to qualify in conformation before becoming a full Champion. A Border Collie that earns the title of Obedience Champion (Ob Ch.) must also qualify in the conformation ring before becoming a Champion.

The U.S. doesn't have a designation full Champion but does award for Dual and Triple Champions. The Dual Champion must be a Champion of Record, and either Champion Tracker, Herding Champion, Obedience Trial Champion or Field Champion. Any dog that has been awarded the titles of Champion of Record, and any two of the following: Champion Tracker, Herding Champion, Obedience Trial Champion or Field Champion, may be designated as a Triple Champion.

In conformation, your dog is judged by how closely he conforms to the breed standard. Pictured is Kombinalong Twycas Super.

The shows in England seem to put more emphasis on breeder judges than those in the U.S. There is much competition within the breeds. Therefore the quality of the individual breeds should be very good. In the United States we tend to have more "all around judges" (those that judge multiple breeds) and use the breeder judges at the specialty shows. Breeder judges are more familiar with their own breed since they are actively breeding that breed or did so at one time. Americans emphasize Group and Best in Show wins and promote them accordingly.

The shows in England can be very large and extend over several days, with the Groups being scheduled on different days. Though multi-day shows are not common in the U.S., there are cluster shows, where several different clubs will use the same show site over consecutive days.

Westminster Kennel Club is our most prestigious show although the entry is limited to 2500. In recent years, entry has been limited to Champions. This show is more formal than the majority of the shows with the judges wearing formal attire and the handlers fashionably dressed. In most instances the quality of the dogs is superb. After all, it is a show of Champions. It is a good show to study the AKC registered breeds and is by far the most exciting—especially since it is televised! WKC is one of the few shows in this country that is still benched. This means the dog must be in his benched area during the show hours except when he is being groomed, in the ring, or being exercised.

Typically, the handlers are very particular about their appearances. They are careful not to wear something that will detract from their dog but will perhaps enhance it. American ring procedure is quite formal compared to that of other countries. There is a certain etiquette expected between the judge and exhibitor and among the other exhibitors. Of course it is not always the case but the judge is supposed to be polite, not engaging in small talk or acknowledging how well he knows the handler. There is a more informal and relaxed atmosphere at the shows in other countries. For instance, the dress code is more casual. I can see where this might be more fun for the exhibitor and especially for the novice. The U.S. is very handler-oriented in many of the breeds. It is true, in most instances, that the experienced professional handler can present the dog better and will have a feel for what a judge likes.

In England, Crufts is The Kennel Club's own show and is most assuredly the largest dog show in the world. They've

Although they are young now, perhaps these Australian Cattle Dog puppies will grow into champion show dogs.

been known to have an entry of nearly 20,000, and the show lasts four days. Entry is only gained by qualifying through winning in specified classes at another Championship Show. Westminster is strictly conformation, but Crufts exhibitors and

This pair of Australian Cattle Dogs awaits their turn in the show ring.

spectators enjoy not only conformation but obedience, agility and a multitude of exhibitions as well. Obedience was admitted in 1957 and agility in 1983.

If you are handling your own dog, please give some consideration to your apparel. For sure the dress code at matches is more informal than the point shows. However, you should wear something a little more appropriate than beach attire or ragged jeans and bare feet. If you check out the handlers and see what is presently fashionable, you'll catch on. Men usually dress with a shirt and tie and a nice sports coat. Whether you are male or female, you will want to wear comfortable clothes and shoes. You need to be able to run with your dog and you certainly don't want to take a chance of falling and hurting yourself. Heaven forbid, if nothing else, you'll upset your dog. Women usually wear a dress or two-piece outfit, preferably with pockets to carry bait, comb, brush, etc. In this case men are the lucky ones with all their pockets. Ladies, think about where your dress will be if you need to kneel on the floor and also think about running. Does it allow freedom to do so?

You need to take along dog; crate; ex pen (if you use one); extra newspaper; water pail and water; all required grooming equipment, including hair dryer and extension cord; table; chair for you; bait for dog and lunch for you and friends; and, last but not least, clean up materials, such as plastic bags, paper towels, and perhaps a bath towel and some shampoo—just in case. Don't forget your entry confirmation and directions to the show.

If you are showing in obedience, then you will want to wear pants. Many of our top obedience handlers wear pants that are color-coordinated with their dogs. The philosophy is that imperfections in the black dog will be less obvious next to your black pants.

Whether you are showing in conformation, Junior Showmanship or obedience, you need to watch the clock and be sure you are not late. It is customary to pick up your conformation armband a few minutes before the start of the class. They will not wait for you and if you are on the show grounds and not in the ring, you will upset everyone. It's a little more complicated picking up your obedience armband if you show later in the class. If you have not picked up your armband and they get to your number, you may not be allowed to show. It's best to pick up your armband early, but then you may show earlier than expected if other handlers don't pick up. Customarily all conflicts should be discussed with the judge prior to the start of the class.

With persistence, patience, and praise, your versatile Australian Cattle Dog will become a well-trained and obedient companion.

Junior Showmanship

The Junior Showmanship Class is a wonderful way to build self confidence even if there are no aspirations of staying with the dog-show game later in life. Frequently, Junior Showmanship becomes the background of those who become successful exhibitors/handlers in the future. In some instances it is taken very seriously, and success is measured in terms of wins. The Junior Handler is judged solely on his ability and skill in presenting his dog. The dog's conformation is not to be considered by the judge. Even so the condition and grooming of the dog may be a reflection upon the handler.

Usually the matches and point shows include different classes. The Junior Handler's dog may be entered in a breed or

Young James Hannan gets an early start on practicing for junior handling with "Doc."

obedience class and even shown by another person in that class. Junior Showmanship classes are usually divided by age and perhaps sex. The age is determined by the handler's age on the day of the show.

CANINE GOOD CITIZEN

The AKC sponsors a program to encourage dog owners to train their dogs. Local clubs perform the pass/fail tests, and dogs who pass are awarded a Canine Good Citizen Certificate. Proof of vaccination is required at the time of participation. The test includes:

1. Accepting a friendly stranger.
2. Sitting politely for petting.
3. Appearance and grooming.
4. Walking on a loose leash.
5. Walking through a crowd.
6. Sit and down on command/staying in place.
7. Come when called.
8. Reaction to another dog.
9. Reactions to distractions.
10. Supervised separation.

If more effort was made by pet owners to accomplish these exercises, fewer dogs would be cast off to the humane shelter.

OBEDIENCE

Obedience is necessary, without a doubt, but it can also become a wonderful hobby or even an obsession. Obedience classes and competition can provide wonderful companionship, not only with your dog but with your classmates or fellow competitors. It is always gratifying to discuss your dog's problems with others who have had similar experiences. The AKC acknowledged Obedience around 1936, and it has changed

Margaret Price gives the next command to her apt pupil, Tirlta Rising Star.

tremendously even though many of the exercises are basically the same. Today, obedience competition is just that—very competitive. Even so, it is possible for every obedience exhibitor to come home a winner (by earning qualifying scores) even though he/she may not earn a placement in the class.

Every Australian Cattle Dog is a champion in his owner's eyes and this little guy is sure of it!

Most of the obedience titles are awarded after earning three qualifying scores (legs) in the appropriate class under three different judges. These classes offer a perfect score of 200, which is extremely rare. Each of the class exercises has its own point value. A leg is earned after receiving a score of at least 170 and at least 50 percent of the points available in each exercise. The titles are:

Companion Dog—CD
This is called the Novice Class and the exercises are:

1. Heel on leash and figure 8	40 points
2. Stand for examination	30 points
3. Heel free	40 points
4. Recall	30 points
5. Long sit—one minute	30 points
6. Long down—three minutes	30 points
Maximum total score	200 points

Companion Dog Excellent—CDX
This is the Open Class and the exercises are:

1. Heel off leash and figure 8	40 points
2. Drop on recall	30 points
3. Retrieve on flat	20 points
4. Retrieve over high jump	30 points
5. Broad jump	20 points
6. Long sit—three minutes (out of sight)	30 points
7. Long down—five minutes (out of sight)	30 points
Maximum total score	200 points

Utility Dog–UD
The Utility Class exercises are:

1.Signal Exercise	40 points
2.Scent discrimination-Article 1	30 points
3.Scent discrimination-Article 2	30 points
4.Directed retrieve	30 points
5.Moving stand and examination	30 points
6.Directed jumping	40 points
Maximum total score	200 points

After achieving the UD title, you may feel inclined to go after the UDX and/or OTCh. The UDX (Utility Dog Excellent) title went into effect in January 1994. It is not easily attained. The title requires qualifying simultaneously ten times in Open B and Utility B but not necessarily at consecutive shows.

Agility competitions are growing in popularity. This Australian Cattle Dog easily sails over the bar jump in an agility trial.

The OTCh (Obedience Trial Champion) is awarded after the dog has earned his UD and then goes on to earn 100 championship points, a first place in Utility, a first place in Open and another first place in either class. The placements must be won under three different judges at all-breed obedience trials. The points are determined by the number of dogs competing in the Open B and Utility B classes. The OTCh title precedes the dog's name.

Obedience matches (AKC Sanctioned, Fun, and Show and Go) are usually available. Usually they are sponsored by the local obedience clubs. When preparing an obedience dog for a title, you will find matches very helpful. Fun Matches and Show and Go Matches are more lenient in allowing you to make corrections in the ring. This type of training is usually very necessary for the Open and Utility Classes. AKC Sanctioned Obedience Matches do not allow corrections in the ring since they must abide by the AKC Obedience Regulations. If you are interested in showing in obedience, then you should contact the AKC for a copy of the Obedience Regulations.

TRACKING
Tracking is officially classified obedience. There are three tracking titles available: Tracking Dog (TD), Tracking Dog

Excellent (TDX), Variable Surface Tracking (VST). If all three tracking titles are obtained, then the dog officially becomes a CT (Champion Tracker). The CT will go in front of the dog's name.

A TD may be earned anytime and does not have to follow the other obedience titles. There are many exhibitors that prefer tracking to obedience, and there are others who do both.

Tracking Dog–TD

A dog must be certified by an AKC tracking judge that he is ready to perform in an AKC test. The AKC can provide the names of tracking judges in your area that you can contact for certification. Depending on where you live, you may have to travel a distance if there is no local tracking judge. The certification track will be equivalent to a regular AKC track. A regulation track must be 440 to 500 yards long with at least two right-angle turns out in the open. The track will be aged 30 minutes to two hours. The handler has two starting flags at the beginning of the track to indicate the direction started. The dog works on a harness and 40-foot lead and must work at least 20 feet in front of the handler. An article (either a dark glove or wallet) will be dropped at the end of the track, and the dog must indicate it but not necessarily retrieve it.

People always ask what the dog tracks. Initially, the beginner on the short-aged track tracks the tracklayer. Eventually the dog learns to track the disturbed vegetation and learns to differentiate between tracks. Getting started with tracking requires reading the AKC regulations and a good book on tracking plus finding other tracking enthusiasts. Work on

the buddy system. That is—lay tracks for each other so you can practice blind tracks. It is possible to train on your own, but if you are a beginner, it is a lot more entertaining to track with a buddy. It's rewarding seeing the dog use his natural ability.

The Australian Cattle Dog is an energetic and intelligent dog and will be most happy when active.

Agility is just one of the many activities in which Australian Cattle Dogs can demonstrate their athletic and competitive prowess.

Tracking Dog Excellent–TDX

The TDX track is 800 to 1000 yards long and is aged three to five hours. There will be five to seven turns. An article is left at the starting flag, and three other articles must be indicated on the track. There is only one flag at the start, so it is a blind start. Approximately one and a half hours after the track is laid, two tracklayers will cross over the track at two different places to test the dog's ability to stay with the original track. There will be at least two obstacles on the track such as a change of cover, fences, creeks, ditches, etc. The dog must have a TD before entering a TDX. There is no certification required for a TDX.

AGILITY

Agility was first introduced by John Varley in England at the Crufts Dog Show, February 1978, but Peter Meanwell, competitor and judge, actually developed the idea. It was officially recognized in the early '80s. Agility is extremely popular in England and Canada and growing in popularity in the U.S. The AKC acknowledged agility in August 1994. Dogs must be at least 12 months of age to be entered. It is a fascinating sport that the dog, handler and spectators enjoy to the utmost. Agility is a spectator sport! The dog performs off lead. The handler either runs with his dog or positions himself on the course and directs his dog with verbal and hand signals over a timed course over or through a variety of obstacles

UCDX Mr. Here Comes Trouble CDX, TDX, BAD, CGC, QW, demonstrates the athleticism for which the Australian Cattle Dog is known.

including a time out or pause. One of the main drawbacks to agility is finding a place to train. The obstacles take up a lot of space and it is very time consuming to put up and take down courses.

The titles earned at AKC agility trials are Novice Agility Dog (NAD), Open Agility Dog (OAD), Agility Dog Excellent (ADX), and Master Agility Excellent (MAX). In order to acquire an agility title, a dog must earn a qualifying score in its respective class on three separate occasions under two different judges. The MAX will be awarded after earning ten qualifying scores in the Agility Excellent Class.

PERFORMANCE TESTS

During the last decade the American Kennel Club has promoted performance tests–those events that test the different breeds' natural abilities. This type of event encourages a handler to devote even more time to his dog and retain the natural instincts of his breed heritage. It is an important part of the wonderful world of dogs.

Herding Titles

For all Herding breeds and Rottweilers and Samoyeds.

Entrants must be at least nine months of age and dogs with limited registration (ILP) are

In many places, the Australian Cattle Dog still works at herding cattle, the task for which he was originally bred.

eligible. The Herding program is divided into Testing and Trial sections. The goal is to demonstrate proficiency in herding livestock in diverse situations. The titles offered are Herding Started (HS), Herding Intermediate (HI), and Herding Excellent (HX). Upon completion of the HX a Herding Championship may be earned after accumulating 15 championship points.

The above information has been taken from the AKC Guidelines for the appropriate events.

GENERAL INFORMATION

Obedience, tracking and agility allow the purebred dog with an Indefinite Listing Privilege (ILP) number or a limited registration to be exhibited and earn titles. Application must be made to the AKC for an ILP number.

The American Kennel Club publishes a monthly *Events* magazine that is part of the *Gazette*, their official journal for the sport of purebred dogs. The *Events* section lists upcoming shows and the secretary or superintendent for them. The majority of the conformation shows in the U.S. are overseen by licensed superintendents. Generally the entry closing date is approximately two-and-a-half weeks before the actual show. Point shows are fairly expensive, while the match shows cost about one third of the point show entry fee. Match shows usually take entries the day of the show but some are pre-entry. The best way to find match show information is through your local kennel club. Upon asking, the AKC can provide you with a list of superintendents, and you can write and ask to be put on their mailing lists.

One-year-old Twyn Blu Bankbuster, or "Floyd" to his friends, is in all his glory doing what he was bred to do— herding!

Obedience trial and tracking test information is available through the AKC. Frequently these events are not superintended, but put on by the host club. Therefore you would make the entry with the event's secretary.

As you have read, there are numerous activities you can share with your dog.

Marilyn Hahn and an Australian Cattle Dog pupil enjoy a herding training session.

The Australian Cattle Dog's athletic build and innate intelligence make him a natural for successful agility competition.

Regardless what you do, it does take teamwork. Your dog can only benefit from your attention and training. We hope this chapter has enlightened you and hope, if nothing else, you will attend a show here and there. Perhaps you will start with a puppy kindergarten class, and who knows where it may lead!

HEALTH CARE

Veterinary medicine has become far more sophisticated than what was available to our ancestors. This can be attributed to the increase in household pets and consequently the demand for better care for them. Also human medicine has become far more complex. Today diagnostic testing in veterinary medicine parallels human diagnostics. Because of better technology we can expect our pets to live healthier lives thereby increasing their life spans.

THE FIRST CHECK UP

You will want to take your new puppy/dog in for its first check up within 48 to 72 hours after acquiring it. Many breeders strongly recommend this check up and so do the humane shelters. A puppy/dog can appear healthy but it may have a serious problem that is not apparent to the layman. Most pets have some type of a minor flaw that may never cause a real problem.

Unfortunately if he/she should have a serious problem, you will want to consider the consequences of keeping the pet and the attachments that will be formed, which may be broken prematurely. Keep in mind there are many healthy dogs looking for good homes.

This first check up is a good time to establish yourself with the veterinarian and learn the office policy regarding their hours and how they handle emergencies. Usually the breeder or another conscientious pet owner is a good reference for locating a capable veterinarian. You should be aware that not all veterinarians give the same quality of service. Please do not

Well-cared-for puppies are plump and content right from birth. Responsible breeders take great pains to ensure the health of their breeding stock.

Breeding should only be attempted by someone who is conscientious, knowledgeable, and willing to take responsibility for the dogs and new puppies involved.

make your selection on the least expensive clinic, as they may be short changing your pet. There is the possibility that eventually it will cost you more due to improper diagnosis, treatment, etc. If you are selecting a new veterinarian, feel free to ask for a tour of the clinic. You should inquire about making an appointment for a tour since all clinics are working clinics, and therefore may not be available all day for sightseers. You may worry less if you see where your pet will be spending the day if he ever needs to be hospitalized.

THE PHYSICAL EXAM

Your veterinarian will check your pet's overall condition, which includes listening to the heart; checking the respiration; feeling the abdomen, muscles and joints; checking the mouth, which includes the gum color and signs of gum disease along with plaque buildup; checking the ears for signs of an infection or ear mites; examining the eyes; and, last but not least, checking

the condition of the skin and coat.

He should ask you questions regarding your pet's eating and elimination habits and invite you to relay your questions. It is a good idea to prepare a list so as not to forget anything. He should discuss the proper diet and the quantity to be fed. If this should differ from your breeder's recommendation, then you should convey to him the breeder's choice and see if he approves. If he recommends changing the diet, then this should be done over a few days so as not to cause a gastrointestinal upset. It is customary to take in a fresh stool sample (just a small amount) for a test for intestinal parasites. It must be fresh, preferably within 12 hours, since the eggs hatch quickly and after hatching will not be observed under the microscope. If your pet isn't obliging then, usually the technician can take one in the clinic.

There is nothing more endearing then the relationship between a mother and her young. As puppies, Australian Cattle Dogs rely on their mothers to provide for all of their needs.

IMMUNIZATIONS

It is important that you take your puppy/dog's vaccination record with you on your first visit. In case of a puppy, presumably the breeder has seen to the vaccinations up to the time you acquired custody. Veterinarians differ in their vaccination protocol. It is not unusual for your puppy to have received vaccinations for distemper, hepatitis, leptospirosis, parvovirus and parainfluenza every two to three weeks from the age of five or six weeks. Usually this is a combined injection and is typically called the DHLPP. The DHLPP is given through at least 12 to 14 weeks of age, and it is customary to continue with another parvovirus vaccine at 16 to 18 weeks. You may wonder why so many immunizations are necessary. No one knows for sure when the puppy's maternal antibodies are gone, although it is

For the sake of your puppy as well as the health of your family, you should bring your new Cattle Dog to the veterinarian within three days of his arrival at your home.

customarily accepted that distemper antibodies are gone by 12 weeks. Usually parvovirus antibodies are gone by 16 to 18 weeks of age. However, it is possible for the maternal antibodies to be gone at a much earlier age or even a later age. Therefore immunizations are started at an early age. The vaccine will not give immunity as long as there are maternal antibodies.

The rabies vaccination is given at three or six months of age depending on your local laws. A vaccine for bordetella (kennel cough) is advisable and can be given anytime from the age of five weeks. The coronavirus is not commonly given unless there is a problem locally. The Lyme vaccine is necessary in endemic areas. Lyme disease has been reported in 47 states.

Distemper

This is virtually an incurable disease. If the dog recovers, he is subject to severe nervous disorders. The virus attacks every tissue in the body and resembles a bad cold with a fever. It can cause a runny nose and eyes and cause gastrointestinal disorders, including a poor appetite, vomiting and diarrhea. The virus is carried by raccoons, foxes, wolves, mink and other dogs. Unvaccinated youngsters and senior citizens are very susceptible. This is still a common disease.

Hepatitis

This is a virus that is most serious in very young dogs. It is spread by contact with an infected animal or its stool or urine. The virus affects the liver and kidneys and is characterized by high fever, depression and lack of appetite. Recovered animals may be afflicted with chronic illnesses.

Leptospirosis

This is a bacterial disease transmitted by contact with the urine of an infected dog, rat or other wildlife. It produces severe symptoms of fever, depression, jaundice and internal bleeding and was fatal before the vaccine was developed. Recovered dogs can be carriers, and the disease can be transmitted from dogs to humans.

Parvovirus

This was first noted in the late 1970s and is still a fatal disease. However, with proper vaccinations, early diagnosis and prompt treatment, it is a manageable disease. It attacks the bone marrow and intestinal tract. The symptoms include depression, loss of appetite, vomiting, diarrhea and collapse. Immediate medical attention is of the essence.

Rabies
This is shed in the saliva and is carried by raccoons, skunks, foxes, other dogs and cats. It attacks nerve tissue, resulting in paralysis and death. Rabies can be transmitted to people and is virtually always fatal. This disease is reappearing in the suburbs.

Bordetella (Kennel Cough)
The symptoms are coughing, sneezing, hacking and retching accompanied by nasal discharge usually lasting from a few days to several weeks. There are several disease-producing organisms responsible for this disease. The present vaccines are helpful but do not protect for all the strains. It usually is not life threatening but in some instances it can progress to a serious bronchopneumonia. The disease is highly contagious. The vaccination should be given routinely for dogs that come in contact with other dogs, such as through boarding, training class or visits to the groomer.

All Australian Cattle Dog puppies are cute, but not all are of breeding quality. Reputable breeders will often sell pet-quality dogs on the condition that they are spayed or neutered.

Coronavirus

This is usually self limiting and not life threatening. It was first noted in the late '70s about a year before parvovirus. The virus produces a yellow/brown stool and there may be depression, vomiting and diarrhea.

Lyme Disease

This was first diagnosed in the United States in 1976 in Lyme, CT in people who lived in close proximity to the deer tick. Symptoms may include acute lameness, fever, swelling of joints and loss of appetite. Your veterinarian can advise you if you live in an endemic area.

After your puppy has completed his puppy vaccinations, you will continue to booster the DHLPP once a year. It is customary to booster the rabies one year after the first vaccine and then, depending on where you live, it should be boostered every year or every three years. This depends on your local laws. The Lyme and corona vaccines are boostered annually and it is recommended that the bordetella be boostered every six to eight months.

ANNUAL VISIT

I would like to impress the importance of the annual check up, which would include the booster vaccinations, check for intestinal parasites and test for heartworm. Today in our very busy world it is rush, rush and see "how much you can get for how little." Unbelievably, some non-veterinary businesses have entered into the vaccination business. More harm than good can come to your dog

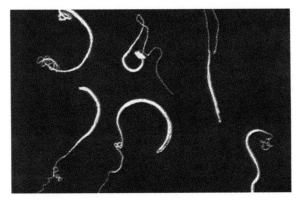

Whipworms are hard to detect, and it is a job best left to a veterinarian. Pictured here are adult whipworms.

through improper vaccinations, possibly from inferior vaccines and/or the wrong schedule. More than likely you truly care about your companion dog and over the years you have devoted much time and expense to his well being. Perhaps you are unaware that a vaccination is not just a vaccination. There is more involved. Please, please follow through with regular physical examinations. It is so important for your veterinarian to know

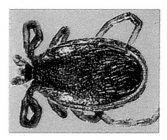

The deer tick is the most common carrier of Lyme disease. Photo courtesy of Virbac Laboratories, Inc., Fort Worth, Texas.

your dog and this is especially true during middle age through the geriatric years. More than likely your older dog will require more than one physical a year. The annual physical is good preventive medicine. Through early diagnosis and subsequent treatment your dog can maintain a longer and better quality of life.

INTESTINAL PARASITES

Hookworms

These are almost microscopic intestinal worms that can cause anemia and therefore serious problems, including death, in young puppies. Hookworms can be transmitted to humans through penetration of the skin. Puppies may be born with them.

Roundworms

These are spaghetti-like worms that can cause a potbellied appearance and dull coat along with more severe symptoms, such as vomiting, diarrhea and coughing. Puppies acquire these while in the mother's uterus and through lactation. Both hookworms and roundworms may be acquired through ingestion.

Whipworms

These have a three-month life cycle and are not acquired through the dam. They cause intermittent diarrhea usually with mucus. Whipworms are possibly the most difficult worm to eradicate. Their eggs are very resistant to most environmental factors and can last for years until the proper conditions enable them to mature. Whipworms are seldom seen in the stool.

Intestinal parasites are more prevalent in some areas than others. Climate, soil and contamination are big factors contributing to the incidence of intestinal parasites. Eggs are passed in the stool, lay on the ground and then become infective in a certain number of days. Each of the above worms has a different life cycle. Your best chance of becoming and remaining worm-free is to always pooper-scoop your yard. A fenced-in yard keeps stray dogs out, which is certainly helpful.

I would recommend having a fecal examination on your dog twice a year or more often if there is a problem. If your dog has a positive fecal sample, then he will be given the appropriate medication and you

The Australian Cattle Dog puppy should be energetic and alert. Any changes in his activity should be brought to your veterinarian's attention immediately.

will be asked to bring back another stool sample in a certain period of time (depending on the type of worm) and then be rewormed. This process goes on until he has at least two negative samples. The different types of worms require different medications. You will be wasting your money and doing your dog an injustice by buying over-the-counter medication without first consulting your veterinarian.

Dirofilaria—adult worms in the heart of a dog. Courtesy of Merck AgVet.

OTHER INTERNAL PARASITES

Coccidiosis and Giardiasis

These protozoal infections usually affect puppies, especially in places where large numbers of puppies are brought together. Older dogs may harbor these infections but do not show signs unless they are stressed. Symptoms include diarrhea, weight loss and lack of appetite. These infections are not always apparent in the fecal examination.

Tapeworms

Seldom apparent on fecal floatation, they are diagnosed frequently as rice-like segments around the dog's anus and the base of the tail. Tapeworms are long, flat and ribbon like, sometimes several feet in length, and made up of many segments about five-eighths of an inch long. The two most common types of tapeworms found in the dog are:

(1) First the larval form of the flea tapeworm parasite must mature in an intermediate host, the flea, before it can become infective. Your dog acquires this by ingesting the flea through licking and chewing.

(2) Rabbits, rodents and certain large game animals serve as intermediate hosts for other species of tapeworms. If your dog should eat one of these infected hosts, then he can acquire tapeworms.

HEARTWORM DISEASE

This is a worm that resides in the heart and adjacent blood vessels of the lung that produces microfilaria, which circulate in the bloodstream. It is possible for a dog to be infected with any number of worms from one to a hundred that can be 6 to 14 inches long. It is a life-threatening disease, expensive to treat and easily prevented. Depending on where you live, your veterinarian may recommend a preventive year-round and either an annual or semiannual blood test. The most common preventive is given once a month.

EXTERNAL PARASITES

Fleas

These pests are not only the dog's worst enemy but also enemy to the owner's pocketbook. Preventing is less expensive than treating, but regardless we'd prefer to spend our money elsewhere. Likely, the majority of our dogs are allergic to the bite of a flea, and in many cases it only takes one flea bite. The protein in the flea's saliva is the culprit. Allergic dogs have a reaction, which usually results in a "hot spot." More than likely such a reaction will involve a trip to the veterinarian for treatment. Yes, prevention is less expensive. Fortunately today there are several good products available.

If there is a flea infestation, no one product is going to correct the problem. Not only will the dog require treatment so will the environment. In general flea collars are not very effective although there is now available an "egg" collar that will kill the eggs on the dog. Dips are the most economical but they are messy. There are some effective shampoos and treatments available through pet shops and veterinarians. An oral tablet arrived on the

Regular medical care is extremely important throughout your Australian Cattle Dog's life. Vaccination boosters and physical exams are part of your dog's lifelong maintenance.

American market in 1995 and was popular in Europe the previous year. It sterilizes the female flea but will not kill adult fleas. Therefore the tablet, which is given monthly, will decrease the flea population but is not a "cure-all." Those dogs that suffer from flea-bite allergy will still be subjected to the bite of the flea.

It is important that every puppy gets enough rest to ensure his good health—looks like this little guy is ready for a nap!

Dogs are a very important part of their owner's lives, and the bond between humans and animals is a strong one.

Another popular parasiticide is permethrin, which is applied to the back of the dog in one or two places depending on the dog's weight. This product works as a repellent causing the flea to get "hot feet" and jump

off. Do not confuse this product with some of the organophosphates that are also applied to the dog's back. Some products are not usable on young puppies. Treating fleas should be done under your veterinarian's guidance. Frequently it is necessary to combine products and the layman does not have the knowledge regarding possible toxicities. It is hard to believe but there are a few dogs that do have a natural resistance to fleas. Nevertheless it would be wise to treat all pets at the same time. Don't forget your cats. Cats just love to prowl the neighborhood and consequently return with unwanted guests.

Adult fleas live on the dog but their eggs drop off the dog into the environment. There they go through four larval stages before reaching adulthood, and thereby are able to jump back on the poor unsuspecting dog. The cycle resumes and takes between 21 to 28 days under ideal conditions. There are environmental products available that will kill both the adult fleas and the larvae.

Your Australian Cattle Dog puppy should be bright-eyed, healthy, and interested in the world around him.

There's no denying that this little guy is adorable, but it is important to remember that taking care of a puppy means a lot of time and work for you.

Ticks

Ticks carry Rocky Mountain Spotted Fever, Lyme disease and can cause tick paralysis. They should be removed with tweezers, trying to pull out the head. The jaws carry disease. There is a tick preventive collar that does an excellent job. The ticks automatically back out on those dogs wearing collars.

Sarcoptic Mange

This is a mite that is difficult to find on skin scrapings. The pinnal reflex is a good indicator of this disease. Rub the ends of the pinna (ear) together and the dog will start scratching with his foot. Sarcoptes are highly contagious to other dogs and to humans although they do not live long on humans. They cause intense itching.

Demodectic Mange

This is a mite that is passed from the dam to her puppies. It affects youngsters age three to ten months. Diagnosis is confirmed by skin scraping. Small areas of alopecia around the eyes, lips and/or forelegs become visible. There is little itching unless there is a secondary bacterial infection. Some breeds are afflicted more than others.

Cheyletiella

This causes intense itching and is diagnosed by skin scraping. It lives in the outer layers of the skin of dogs, cats, rabbits and humans. Yellow-gray scales may be found on the back and the rump, top of the head and the nose.

To Breed or Not To Breed

More than likely your breeder has requested that you have your puppy neutered or spayed. Your breeder's request is based on what is healthiest for your dog and what is most beneficial for your breed. Experienced and conscientious breeders devote many years into developing a bloodline. In order to do this, he makes every effort to plan each breeding in regard to conformation, temperament and health. This type of breeder does his best to perform the necessary testing (i.e., OFA, CERF, testing for inherited blood disorders,

This protective mother checks up on her puppy-sitter, Rick Williams, and his two sleeping charges.

thyroid, etc.). Testing is expensive and sometimes very disheartening when a favorite dog doesn't pass his health tests. The health history pertains not only to the breeding stock but to the immediate ancestors. Reputable breeders do not want their offspring to be bred indiscriminately. Therefore you may be asked to neuter or spay your puppy. Of course there is always the exception, and your breeder may agree to let you breed your dog under his direct supervision. This is an important concept. More and more effort is being made to breed healthier dogs.

Spay/Neuter

There are numerous benefits of performing this surgery at six months of age. Unspayed females are subject to mammary

At only two weeks of age, this little guy is already all decked out in his Sunday best!

and ovarian cancer. In order to prevent mammary cancer she must be spayed prior to her first heat cycle. Later in life, an unspayed female may develop a pyometra (an infected uterus), which is definitely life threatening.

Spaying is performed under a general anesthetic and is easy on the young dog. As you might expect it is a little harder on the older dog, but that is no reason to deny her the surgery. The surgery removes the ovaries and uterus. It is important to remove all the ovarian tissue. If some is left behind, she could remain attractive to males. In order to view the ovaries, a reasonably long incision is necessary. An ovariohysterectomy is considered major surgery.

Neutering the male at a young age will inhibit some characteristic male behavior that owners frown upon. Some boys will not hike their legs and mark territory if they are neutered at six months of age. Also neutering at a young age has hormonal benefits, lessening the chance of hormonal aggressiveness.

Surgery involves removing the testicles but leaving the scrotum. If there should be a retained testicle, then he definitely needs to be neutered before the age of two or three years. Retained testicles can develop into cancer. Unneutered males are at risk for testicular

It is important not to leave your puppy unoccupied for long periods of time. A puppy needs stimulation and activity to develop into a well-socialized adult.

cancer, perineal fistulas, perianal tumors and fistulas and prostatic disease.

Intact males and females are prone to housebreaking accidents. Females urinate frequently before, during and after heat cycles, and males tend to mark territory if there is a female in heat. Males may show the same behavior if there is a visiting dog or guests.

Surgery involves a sterile operating procedure equivalent to human surgery. The incision site is shaved, surgically scrubbed and draped. The veterinarian wears a sterile surgical gown, cap, mask and gloves. Anesthesia should be monitored by a registered technician. It is customary for the veterinarian to recommend a pre-anesthetic blood screening, looking for metabolic problems and a ECG rhythm strip to check for normal heart function. Today anesthetics are equal to human anesthetics, which enables your dog to walk out of the clinic the same day as surgery.

Some folks worry about their dog gaining weight after being neutered or spayed. This is usually not the case. It is true that some dogs may be less active so they could develop a problem, but most dogs are just as active as they were before surgery. However, if your dog should begin to gain, then you need to decrease his food and see to it that he gets a little more exercise.

MEDICAL PROBLEMS

Anal Sacs

These are small sacs on either side of the rectum that can cause the dog discomfort when they are full. They should

Look at those sad puppy eyes! Be sure to provide your Australian Cattle Dog puppy with regular veterinary checkups and inoculations.

empty when the dog has a bowel movement. Symptoms of inflammation or impaction are excessive licking under the tail and/or a bloody or sticky discharge from the anal area. Breeders like myself recommend emptying the sacs on a regular schedule when bathing the dog. Many veterinarians prefer this isn't done unless there are symptoms. You can express the sacs by squeezing the two sacs (at the five and seven o'clock positions) in and up toward the anus. Take precautions not to get in the way of the foul-smelling fluid that is expressed. Some dogs object to this procedure so it would be wise to have someone hold the head. Scooting is caused by anal-sac irritation and not worms.

Colitis

The stool may be frank blood or blood tinged and is the result of inflammation of the colon. Colitis, sometimes intermittent, can be the result of stress, undiagnosed whipworms, or perhaps idiopathic (no explainable reason). If intermittent bloody stools are an ongoing problem, you should probably feed a diet higher in fiber. Seek professional help if your dog feels poorly and/or the condition persists.

Conjunctivitis

Many breeds are prone to this problem. The conjunctiva is the pink tissue that lines the inner surface of the eyeball except the clear, transparent cornea. Irritating substances such as bacteria, foreign matter or chemicals can cause it to become reddened and swollen. It is important to keep any hair trimmed from around the eyes. Long hair stays damp and aggravates the problem. Keep the eyes cleaned with warm water and wipe away any matter that has accumulated in the corner of the eyes. If the condition persists, you should see your veterinarian. This problem goes hand in hand with keratoconjunctivitis sicca.

Kuma's bright eyes, clean ears, and pink tongue are all sure signs of a healthy Australian Cattle Dog.

Ear Infection

Otitis externa is an inflammation of the external ear canal that begins at the outside opening of the ear and extends inward to the eardrum. Dogs with pendulous ears are prone to this disease, but isn't it interesting that breeds with upright ears also have a high incidence of problems? Allergies, food and inhalent, along with hormonal problems, such as hypothyroidism, are major contributors to the disease. For those dogs which have recurring problems you need to investigate the underlying cause if you hope to cure them.

Be careful never to get water into the ears. Water provides a great medium for bacteria to grow. If your dog swims or you inadvertently get water into his ears, then use a drying agent. An at-home preparation would be to use equal parts of three-percent hydrogen peroxide and 70-percent rubbing alcohol. Another preparation is equal parts of white vinegar and water. Your veterinarian alternatively can provide a suitable product. When cleaning the ears, be careful of using cotton tip applicators since they make it easy to pack debris down into the canal. Only clean what you can see.

If your dog has an ongoing infection, don't be surprised if your veterinarian recommends sedating him and flushing his ears with a bulb syringe. Sometimes this needs to be done a few times to get the ear clean. The ear must be clean so that medication can come in contact with the canal. Be prepared to return for rechecks until the infection is gone. This may involve more flushings if the ears are very bad.

For chronic or recurring cases, your veterinarian may recommend

Bonding is one of the most important building blocks of your relationship with your Australian Cattle Dog. Mutley and Justice revel in the attention they get from their master.

Encourage your puppy to explore the world around him. New experiences will enrich his life.

thyroid testing, etc., and a hypoallergenic diet for a trial period of 10 to 12 weeks. Depending on your dog, it may be a good idea to see a dermatologist. Ears shouldn't be taken lightly. If the condition gets out of hand, then surgery may be necessary. Please ask your veterinarian to explain proper ear maintenance for your dog.

Flea Bite Allergy

This is the result of a hypersensitivity to the bite of a flea and its saliva. It only takes one bite to cause the dog to chew or scratch himself raw. Your dog may need medical attention to ease his discomfort. You need to clip the hair around the "hot spot" and wash it with a mild soap and water and you may need to do this daily if the area weeps. Apply an antibiotic anti-inflammatory product. Hot spots can occur from other trauma, such as grooming.

Interdigital Cysts

Check for these on your dog's feet if he shows signs of lameness. They are frequently associated with staph infections and can be quite painful. A home remedy is to soak the infected foot in a solution of a half teaspoon of bleach in a couple of quarts of water. Do this two to three times a day for a couple of days. Check with your veterinarian for an alternative remedy; antibiotics usually work well. If there is a recurring problem, surgery may be required.

Lameness

It may only be an interdigital cyst or it could be a mat between the toes, especially if your dog licks his feet. Sometimes it is hard to determine which leg is affected. If he is holding up his leg, then you need to see your veterinarian.

Skin

Frequently poor skin is the result of an allergy to fleas, an inhalant allergy or food allergy. These types of problems usually result in a staph dermatitis. Dogs with food allergy usually show signs of severe itching and scratching. Some dogs with food allergies never once itch. Their only symptom is swelling of the ears with no ear infection. Food allergy may result in recurrent bacterial skin and ear infections. Your veterinarian or dermatologist will recommend a good restricted diet. It is not wise for you to hit and miss with different dog foods. Many of the diets offered over the counter are not the hypoallergenic diet you are led to believe. Dogs acquire allergies through exposure.

Inhalant allergies result in atopy, which causes licking of the feet, scratching the body and rubbing the muzzle. It may be seasonable. Your veterinarian or dermatologist can perform

Spaying/ neutering is often the best option for your family pet. The health benefits are numerous and it will minimize the risk of certain diseases.

intradermal testing for inhalant allergies. If your dog should test positive, then a vaccine may be prepared. The results are very satisfying.

Tonsillitis

Usually young dogs have a higher incidence of this problem than the older ones. The older dogs have built up resistance. It is very contagious.

Herding cattle is hard work! It is important to keep your Australian Cattle Dog in good health so he can do his job.

Australian Cattle Dogs are social creatures and need the company of other dogs. The more time your dog spends with other animals, the better socialized he will become.

Sometimes it is difficult to determine if it is tonsillitis or kennel cough since the symptoms are similar. Symptoms include fever, poor eating, swallowing with difficulty and retching up a white, frothy mucus.

DENTAL CARE for Your Dog's Life

So you've got a new puppy! You also have a new set of puppy teeth in your household. Anyone who has ever raised a puppy is abundantly aware of these new teeth. Your puppy will chew anything it can reach, chase your shoelaces, and play "tear the rag" with any piece of clothing it can find. When puppies are newly born, they have no teeth. At about four weeks of age, puppies of most breeds begin to develop their deciduous or baby teeth. They begin eating semi-solid food, fighting and biting with their litter mates, and learning discipline from

Red Hanky and Yvonne de Jong both pose for the camera and show off their lovely smiles.

their mother. As their new teeth come in, they inflict more pain on their mother's breasts, so her feeding sessions become less frequent and shorter. By six or eight weeks, the mother will start growling to warn her pups when they are fighting too roughly or hurting her as they nurse too much with their new teeth.

Puppies need to chew. It is a necessary part of their physical and mental development. They develop muscles and necessary life skills as they drag objects around, fight over possession, and vocalize alerts and warnings. Puppies chew on things to explore their world. They are using their sense of taste to determine what is food and what is not. How else can they tell an electrical cord from a lizard? At about four months of age, most puppies begin shedding their baby teeth. Often these teeth need some help to come out and make way

If you accustom your Australian Cattle Dog to having his teeth examined at an early age, he will become a far more willing participant in the future.

for the permanent teeth. The incisors (front teeth) will be replaced first. Then, the adult canine or fang teeth erupt. When the baby tooth is not shed before the permanent tooth comes in, veterinarians call it a retained deciduous tooth. This condition will often cause gum infections by trapping hair and debris between the permanent tooth and the retained baby tooth. Nylafloss® is an excellent device for puppies to use. They can toss it, drag it, and chew on the many surfaces it presents. The baby teeth can catch in the nylon material, aiding in their removal. Puppies that have adequate chew toys will have less destructive behavior, develop more physically, and have less chance of retained deciduous teeth.

During the first year, your dog should be seen by your veterinarian at regular intervals. Your veterinarian will let you know when to

The Galileo™ is the toughest nylon bone ever made. It is flavored to appeal to your Australian Cattle Dog and has a relatively soft outer layer. It is a necessary chew toy and doggy pacifier.

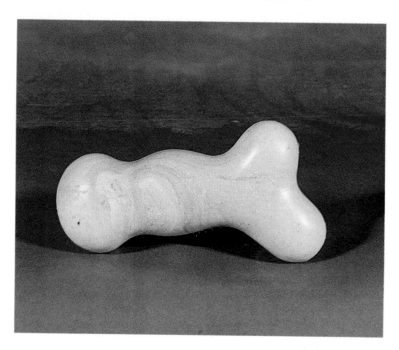

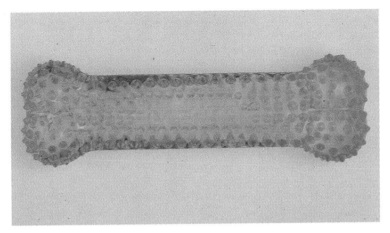

Raised dental tips on the surface of every Plaque Attacker™ bone help to combat plaque and tartar. Safe for aggressive chewers and ruggedly constructed to last, Plaque Attacker dental bones provide hours and hours of tooth-saving enjoyment.

bring in your puppy for vaccinations and parasite examinations. At each visit, your veterinarian should inspect the lips, teeth, and mouth as part of a complete physical examination. You should take some part in the maintenance of your dog's oral health. You should examine your dog's mouth weekly throughout his first year to make sure there are no sores, foreign objects, tooth problems, etc. If your dog drools excessively, shakes its head, or has bad breath, consult your veterinarian. By the time your dog is six months old, the permanent teeth are all in and plaque can start to accumulate on the tooth surfaces. This is when your dog needs to develop good dental-care habits to prevent calculus build-up on its teeth. Brushing is best. That is a fact that cannot be denied. However, some dogs do not like their teeth brushed regularly, or you may not be able to accomplish the task. In that case, you should consider a product that will help prevent plaque and calculus build-up.

The Plaque Attackers® and Galileo Bone® are other excellent choices for the first three years of a dog's life. Their shapes make them interesting for the dog. As the dog chews on them, the solid polyurethane massages the gums which improves the blood circulation to the periodontal tissues. Projections on the chew devices increase the surface and are in contact with the tooth for more efficient cleaning. The unique shape and consistency prevent your dog from exerting excessive force on his own teeth or from breaking off pieces of the bone. If your dog is an aggressive chewer or weighs more than 55 pounds (25 kg), you should consider giving him a Nylabone®, the most durable chew product on the market.

The Gumabones ®, made by the Nylabone Company, is constructed of strong polyurethane, which is softer than nylon. Less powerful chewers prefer the Gumabones® to the Nylabones®. A super option for your dog is the Hercules Bone®, a uniquely shaped bone named after the great Olympian for its exception strength. Like all Nylabone products, they are specially scented to make them attractive to your dog. Ask your veterinarian about these bones and he will validate the good doctor's prescription: Nylabones® not only give your dog a good chewing workout but also help to save your dog's teeth (and even his life, as it protects him from possible fatal periodontal diseases).

By the time dogs are four years old, 75% of them have periodontal disease. It is the most common infection in dogs. Yearly examinations by your veterinarian are essential to maintaining your dog's good health. If your veterinarian detects periodontal disease, he or she may recommend a prophylactic cleaning. To do a thorough cleaning, it will be necessary to put your dog under anesthesia. With modern gas anesthetics and monitoring equipment, the procedure is pretty safe. Your veterinarian will scale the teeth with an ultrasound

*There are all kinds of flying disks for dogs, but only one is made with strength, scent, and originality. The Nylabone Frisbee™ is a must if you want to have this sort of fun with your Australian Cattle Dog. *The trademark Frisbee™ is used under license from Mattel, Inc., California, USA.*

scaler or hand instrument. This removes the calculus from the teeth. If there are calculus deposits below the gum line, the veterinarian will plane the roots to make them smooth. After all of the calculus has been removed, the teeth are

The dental health of your Australian Cattle Dog is very important. Chewing is a necessary function for your dog's well-being.

Brushing your dog's teeth is recommended by every veterinarian. Use the 2-Brush regularly, 3-4 times per week and you may never need your veterinarian to do the job for you.

polished with pumice in a polishing cup. If any medical or surgical treatment is needed, it is done at this time. The final step would be fluoride treatment and your follow-up treatment at home. If the periodontal disease is advanced, the veterinarian may prescribe a medicated

mouth rinse or antibiotics for use at home. Make sure your dog has safe, clean and attractive chew toys and treats. Chooz® treats are another way of using a consumable treat to help keep your dog's teeth clean.

Rawhide is the most popular of all materials for a dog to chew. This has never been good news to dog owners, because rawhide is inherently very dangerous for dogs. Thousands of dogs have died from rawhide, having swallowed the hide after it has become soft and mushy, only to cause stomach and intestinal blockage. A new rawhide product on the market has finally solved the problem of rawhide: molded Roar-Hide® from Nylabone. These are composed of processed, cut up, and melted American rawhide injected into your dog's favorite shape: a dog bone. These dog-safe devices smell and taste like rawhide but don't break up. The ridges on the bones help to fight tartar build-up on the teeth and they last ten times longer than the usual rawhide chews.

As your dog ages, professional examination and cleaning should become more frequent. The mouth should be inspected at least once a year. Your veterinarian may recommend visits every six

To combat boredom and relieve your Australian Cattle Dog's natural desire to chew, there's nothing better than a Roar-Hide™. The Roar-Hide™ is completely edible, high in protein, and low in fat.

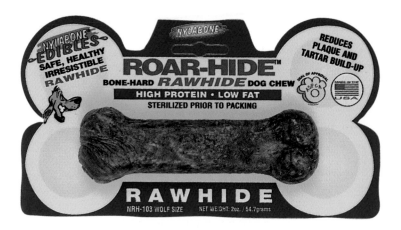

During teething it is important to provide your puppy with things it is appropriate for him to chew on— otherwise he may chomp on your new slippers!

months. In the geriatric patient, organs such as the heart, liver, and kidneys do not function as well as when they were young. Your veterinarian will probably want to test these organs' functions prior to using general anesthesia for dental cleaning. If your dog is a good chewer and you work closely with your veterinarian, your dog can keep all of its teeth all of its life. However, as your dog ages, his sense of smell, sight, and taste will diminish. He may not have the desire to chase, trap or chew his toys. He will also not have the energy to chew for long periods, as arthritis and periodontal disease make chewing painful. This will leave you with more responsibility for keeping his teeth clean and healthy. The dog that would not let you brush his teeth at one year of age, may let you brush his teeth now that he is ten years old.

If you train your dog with good chewing habits as a puppy, he will have healthier teeth throughout his life.

IDENTIFICATION and Finding the Lost Dog

There are several ways of identifying your dog. The old standby is a collar with dog license, rabies, and ID tags. Unfortunately collars have a way of being separated from the dog and tags fall off. We're not suggesting you shouldn't use a collar and tags. If they stay intact and on the dog, they are the quickest way of identification.

For several years owners have been tattooing their dogs. Some tattoos use a number with a registry. Here lies the problem because there are several registries to check. If you wish to tattoo, use your social security number. The humane shelters have the means to trace it. It is usually done on the inside of the rear thigh. The area is first shaved and numbed. There is no pain, although a few dogs do not like the buzzing sound. Occasionally tattooing is not legible and needs to be redone.

The newest method of identification is microchipping. The microchip is a computer chip that is no larger than a grain of rice. The veterinarian implants it by injection between the shoulder blades. The dog feels no discomfort. If your dog is lost and picked up by the humane society, they can trace you by scanning the microchip, which has its own code. Microchip scanners are friendly to other brands of microchips and their

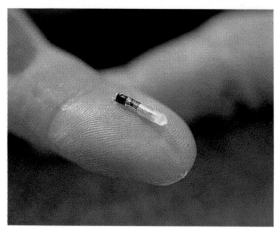

The newest method of identification is micro-chipping. The microchip is no bigger than a grain of rice and is painlessly implanted into the skin.

registries. The microchip comes with a dog tag saying the dog is microchipped. It is the safest way of identifying your dog.

FINDING THE LOST DOG

Australian Cattle Dogs need to be active. Provide yours with a safe outdoor enclosure for playtime.

This little guy looks like he is practicing to become an escape artist. Always make sure that you provide your Australian Cattle Dog with a large fenced-in area to roam in.

I am sure you will agree that there would be little worse than losing your dog. Responsible pet owners rarely lose their dogs. They do not let their dogs run free because they don't want harm to come to them. Not only that but in most, if not all, states there is a leash law.

Beware of fenced-in yards. They can be a hazard. Dogs find ways to escape either over or under the fence. Another fast exit is through the gate that perhaps the neighbor's child left unlocked.

Below is a list that hopefully will be of help to you if you need it. Remember don't give up, keep looking. Your dog is worth your efforts.

Make sure you have a clear recent picture of your Australian Cattle Dog to distribute in case he becomes lost.

1. Contact your neighbors and put flyers with a photo on it in their mailboxes. Information you should include would be the dog's name, breed, sex, color, age, source of identification, when your dog was last seen and where, and your name and phone numbers. It may be helpful to say the dog needs medical care. Offer a *reward*.
2. Check all local shelters daily. It is also possible for your dog to be picked up away from home and end up in an out-of-the-way shelter. Check these too. Go in person. It is not good enough to call. Most shelters are limited on the time they can hold dogs then they are put up for adoption or euthanized. There is the possibility that your dog will not make it to the shelter for several days. Your dog could have been wandering or someone may have tried to keep him.
3. Notify all local veterinarians. Call and send flyers.
4. Call your breeder. Frequently breeders are contacted when one of their breed is found.
5. Contact the rescue group for your breed.
6. Contact local schools—children may have seen your dog.
7. Post flyers at the schools, groceries, gas stations,

convenience stores, veterinary clinics, groomers and any other place that will allow them.
8. Advertise in the newspaper.
9. Advertise on the radio.

When your Australian Cattle Dog spends time outdoors, be sure he wears a collar with tags at all times. This will increase your chances of being reunited should you become separated.

TRAVELING with Your Dog

The earlier you start traveling with your new puppy or dog, the better. He needs to become accustomed to traveling. However, some dogs are nervous riders and become carsick easily. It is helpful if he starts with an empty stomach. Do not despair, as it will go better if you continue taking him with you on short fun rides. How would you feel if every time you rode in the car you stopped at the doctor's for an injection? You would soon dread that nasty car. Older dogs that tend to get carsick may have more of a problem adjusting to traveling. Those dogs that are having a serious problem may benefit from some medication prescribed by the veterinarian.

If your Australian Cattle Dog is a homebody, he may be more comfortable left behind during your travels. In many areas reputable pet sitting services are available.

Do give your dog a chance to relieve himself before getting into the car. It is a good idea to be prepared for a clean up with a leash, paper towels, bag and terry cloth towel.

The safest place for your dog is in a fiberglass crate, although close confinement can promote carsickness in some dogs. If your dog is nervous you can try letting him ride on the seat next to you or in someone's lap.

An alternative to the crate would be to use a car harness made for dogs and/or a safety strap attached to the harness or collar. Whatever you do, do not let your dog ride in the back of a pickup truck unless he is securely tied on a very short lead. I've seen trucks stop quickly and, even though the dog was tied, it fell out and was dragged.

Ride 'em cowboy! At only six weeks of age Turrella Red Teddy is ready to go wherever his equestrian friend takes him.

Another advantage of the crate is that it is a safe place to leave him if you need to run into the store. Otherwise you wouldn't be able to leave the windows down. Keep in mind that while many dogs are overly protective in their crates, this may not be enough to deter dognappers. In some states it is against the law to leave a dog in the car unattended.

Never leave a dog loose in the car wearing a collar and leash. More than one dog has killed himself by hanging. Do not let him put his head out an open window. Foreign debris can be blown into his eyes. When leaving your dog unattended in a car, consider the temperature. It can take less than five minutes to reach temperatures over 100 degrees Fahrenheit.

TRIPS

Perhaps you are taking a trip. Give consideration to what is best for your dog—traveling with you or boarding. When

traveling by car, van or motor home, you need to think ahead about locking your vehicle. In all probability you have many valuables in the car and do not wish to leave it unlocked. Perhaps most valuable and not replaceable is your dog. Give thought to securing your vehicle and providing adequate ventilation for him. Another consideration for you when traveling with your dog is medical problems that may arise and little inconveniences, such as exposure to external parasites. Some areas of the country are quite flea infested. You may want to carry flea spray with you. This is even a good idea when staying in motels. Quite possibly you are not the only occupant of the room.

Your Australian Cattle Dog's well-being is important to you, so be sure to inquire about airline and hotel regulations before making travel plans

Unbelievably many motels and even hotels do allow canine guests, even some very first-class ones. Gaines Pet Foods Corporation publishes *Touring With Towser*, a directory of domestic hotels and motels that accommodate guests with dogs. Their address is Gaines TWT, PO Box 5700, Kankakee, IL, 60902. Call ahead to any motel that you may be considering and see if they accept pets. Sometimes it is necessary to pay a deposit against room damage. The management may feel reassured if you mention that your dog will be crated. If you do travel with your dog, take along plenty of baggies so that you can clean up after him. When we all do our share in cleaning up, we make it possible for motels to continue accepting our pets. As a matter of fact, you should practice cleaning up everywhere you take your dog.

Depending on where your are traveling, you may need an up-to-date health certificate issued by your veterinarian. It is good policy to take along your dog's medical information, which would include the name, address and phone number of your veterinarian, vaccination record, rabies certificate, and any medication he is taking.

It is important to ensure that your Australian Cattle Dog is safely secured in your vehicle before embarking on any outing.

AIR TRAVEL

When traveling by air, you need to contact the airlines to check their policy.

Usually you have to make arrangements up to a couple of weeks in advance for traveling with your dog. The airlines require your dog to travel in an airline approved fiberglass crate. Usually these can be purchased through the airlines but they are also readily available in most pet-supply stores. If your dog is not accustomed to a crate, then it is a good idea to get him acclimated to it before your trip. The day of the actual trip you should withhold water about one hour ahead of departure and no food for about 12 hours. The airlines generally have temperature restrictions, which do not allow pets to travel if it is either too cold or too hot. Frequently these restrictions are based on the temperatures at the departure and arrival airports. It's best to inquire about a health certificate. These usually need to be issued within ten days of departure. You should arrange for non-stop, direct flights and if a commuter plane should be involved, check to see if it will carry dogs. Some don't. The Humane Society of the United States has put together a

Before any car excursion, be sure to allow your Australian Cattle Dog plenty of time outdoors to attend to his needs.

Take along your dog's medical information with you when you travel, especially his vaccination record.

tip sheet for airline traveling. You can receive a copy by sending a self-addressed stamped envelope to:

The Humane Society of the United States
Tip Sheet
2100 L Street NW
Washington, DC 20037.

Regulations differ for traveling outside of the country and are sometimes changed without notice. Well in advance you need to write or call the appropriate consulate or agricultural department for instructions. Some countries have lengthy quarantines (six months), and countries differ in their rabies vaccination requirements. For instance, it may have to be given at least 30 days ahead of your departure.

Do make sure your dog is wearing proper identification including your name, phone number and city. You never know when you might be in an accident and separated from your dog. Or your dog could be frightened and somehow manage to escape and run away.

Another suggestion would be to carry in-case-of-emergency instructions. These would include the address and phone number of a relative or friend, your veterinarian's name, address and phone number, and your dog's medical information.

BOARDING KENNELS

Perhaps you have decided that you need to board your dog. Your veterinarian can recommend a good boarding facility or possibly a pet sitter that will come to your house. It is customary for the boarding kennel to ask for

If you take your Australian Cattle Dog traveling with you often, he will quickly become accustomed to riding in the car, or on the car— whatever the case may be!

proof of vaccination for the DHLPP, rabies and bordetella vaccine. The bordetella should have been given within six months of boarding. This is for your protection. If they do not ask for this proof I would not board at their kennel. Ask about flea control. Those dogs that suffer flea-bite allergy can get in trouble at a boarding kennel. Unfortunately boarding kennels are limited on how much they are able to do.

For more information on pet sitting, contact NAPPS:
National Association of Professional Pet Sitters
1200 G Street, NW
Suite 760
Washington, DC 20005.

Some pet clinics have technicians that pet sit and technicians that board clinic patients in their homes. This may be an alternative for you. Ask your veterinarian if they have an employee that can help you. There is a definite advantage of having a technician care for your dog, especially if your dog is on medication or is a senior citizen.

You can write for a copy of *Traveling With Your Pet* from
ASPCA, Education Department, 441 E. 92nd Street, New York, NY 10128.

A reputable boarding kennel will require that dogs receive the vaccination for kennel cough no less than two weeks before their scheduled stay.

BEHAVIOR and Canine Communication

Studies of the human/animal bond point out the importance of the unique relationships that exist between people and their pets. Those of us who share our lives with pets understand the special part they play through companionship, service and protection. For many, the pet/owner bond goes beyond simple companionship; pets are often considered members of the family. A leading pet food manufacturer recently conducted a nationwide survey of pet owners to gauge just how important pets were in their lives. Here's what they found:

• 76 percent allow their pets to sleep on their beds

Most Australian Cattle Dog owners consider their dogs to be part of their family and include them in all activities.

• 78 percent think of their pets as their children
• 84 percent display photos of their pets, mostly in their homes
• 84 percent think that their pets react to their own emotions
• 100 percent talk to their pets
• 97 percent think that their pets understand what they're saying

Are you surprised?

Senior citizens show more concern for their own eating habits when they have the responsibility of feeding a dog. Seeing that their dog is routinely exercised encourages the owner to think of schedules that otherwise may seem unimportant to the senior citizen. The older owner may be arthritic and feeling poorly but with responsibility for his dog he has a reason to get up and get moving. It is a big plus if his dog is an attention seeker who will demand such from his owner.

There's no telling what your Australian Cattle Dog can accomplish— this fellow seems to be enjoying his career as a word processor!

Over the last couple of decades, it has been shown that pets relieve the stress of those who lead busy lives. Owning a pet has been known to lessen the occurrence of heart attack and stroke.

Many single folks thrive on the companionship of a dog. Lifestyles are very different from a long time ago, and today more individuals seek the single life. However, they receive fulfillment from owning a dog.

Most likely the majority of our dogs live in family environments. The companionship they provide is well worth the effort involved. In my opinion, every child should have the opportunity to have a family dog. Dogs teach responsibility through understanding their care, feelings and even respecting their life cycles. Frequently those children who have not been exposed to dogs grow up afraid of dogs, which isn't good. Dogs sense timidity and some will take advantage of the situation.

Today more dogs are serving as service dogs. Since the origination of the Seeing Eye dogs years ago, we now have trained hearing dogs. Also dogs are trained to provide service for the handicapped and are able to perform many different tasks for their owners. Search and Rescue dogs, with their handlers, are sent throughout the world to assist in recovery of disaster victims. They are life savers.

Therapy dogs are very popular with nursing homes, and some hospitals even allow them to visit. The inhabitants truly look forward to their visits. They wanted and were allowed to have visiting dogs in their beds to hold and love.

Your puppy's relationship with his littermates is an essential one. He will learn to interact with other dogs by playing with his siblings.

Nationally there is a Pet Awareness Week to educate students and others about the value and basic care of our

An Australian Cattle Dog's personality will often be evident in the way she interacts with other animals. Annie and her friend relax on the porch. pets. Many countries take an even greater interest in their pets than Americans do. In those countries the pets are allowed to accompany their owners into restaurants and shops, etc. In the U.S. this freedom is only available to our service dogs. Even so we think very highly of the human/animal bond.

CANINE BEHAVIOR

Canine behavior problems are the number-one reason for pet owners to dispose of their dogs, either through new homes, humane shelters or euthanasia. Unfortunately there are too many owners who are unwilling to devote the necessary time to properly train their dogs. On the other hand, there are those who not only are concerned about inherited health problems but are also aware of the dog's mental stability.

You may realize that a breed and his group relatives (i.e., sporting, hounds, etc.) show tendencies to behavioral characteristics. An experienced breeder can acquaint you with his breed's personality. Unfortunately many breeds are labeled with poor temperaments when actually the breed as a whole is not affected but only a small percentage of individuals within the breed.

Inheritance and environment contribute to the dog's behavior. Some naïve people suggest inbreeding as the cause of bad temperaments. Inbreeding only results in poor behavior if the ancestors carry the trait. If there are excellent temperaments behind the dogs, then inbreeding will promote good temperaments in the offspring. Did you ever consider that inbreeding is

People who are exposed to dogs learn to love, understand, and respect animals.

what sets the characteristics of a breed? A purebred dog is the end result of inbreeding. This does not spare the mixed-breed dog from the same problems. Mixed-breed dogs frequently are the offspring of purebred dogs.

Not too many decades ago most of our dogs led a different lifestyle than what is prevalent today. Usually mom stayed home so the dog had human companionship and someone to discipline it if needed. Not much was expected from the dog. Today's mom works and everyone's life is at a much faster pace.

The dog may have to adjust to being a "weekend" dog. The family is gone all day during the week, and the dog is left to his own devices for entertainment. Some dogs sleep all day waiting for their family to come home and others become

wigwam wreckers if given the opportunity. Crates do ensure the safety of the dog and the house. However, he could become a physically and emotionally cripple if he doesn't get enough exercise and attention. We still appreciate and want the companionship of our dogs although we expect more from them. In many cases we tend to forget dogs are just that—*dogs* not human beings.

A stable, even-tempered Australian Cattle Dog is one that is neither fearful nor aggressive.

SOCIALIZING AND TRAINING

Many prospective puppy buyers lack experience regarding the proper socialization and training needed to develop the type of pet we all desire. In the first 18 months, training does take some work. It is easier to start proper training before there is a problem that needs to be corrected.

The initial work begins with the breeder. The breeder should start socializing the puppy at five to six weeks of age and cannot let up. Human socializing is critical up through 12 weeks of age and likewise important during the following months. The litter should be left together during the first few weeks but it is necessary to separate them by ten weeks of age. Leaving them together after that time will increase competition for litter dominance. If puppies are not socialized with people by 12 weeks of age, they will be timid in later life.

The eight- to ten-week age period is a fearful time for puppies. They need to be handled very gently around children and adults. There should be no harsh discipline during this time. Starting at 14 weeks of age, the puppy begins the juvenile period, which ends when he reaches sexual maturity around six to 14 months of age. During the juvenile period he needs to be introduced to strangers (adults, children and other dogs) on the home property. At sexual maturity he will begin to bark at strangers and become more protective. Males start to lift their legs to urinate but if you desire you can inhibit this behavior by walking your boy on leash away from trees, shrubs, fences, etc.

Perhaps you are thinking about an older puppy. You need to inquire about the puppy's social experience. If he has lived in a kennel, he may have a hard time adjusting to people and environmental stimuli. Assuming he has had a good social upbringing, there are advantages to an older puppy.

Training includes puppy kindergarten and a minimum of one to two basic training classes. During these classes you will learn how to dominate your youngster. This is especially important if you own a large breed of dog. It is somewhat harder, if not nearly impossible, for some owners to be the Alpha figure when their dog towers over them. You will be taught how to properly restrain your dog. This concept is important. Again it puts you in the Alpha position. All dogs need to be restrained many times during their lives. Believe it or not, some of our worst offenders are the eight-week-old puppies that are brought to our clinic. They need to be gently restrained for a nail trim but the way they carry on you would think we were killing them. In comparison, their vaccination is a "piece of cake." When we ask dogs to do something that is not agreeable to them, then their worst comes out. Life will be easier for your dog if you expose him at a young age to the necessities of life—proper behavior and restraint.

UNDERSTANDING THE DOG'S LANGUAGE

Most authorities agree that the dog is a descendent of the wolf. The dog and wolf have similar traits. For instance both are pack oriented and prefer not to be isolated for long periods of time. Another characteristic is that the dog, like the wolf, looks to the leader—Alpha—for direction. Both the wolf and the dog communicate through body language, not only within their pack but with outsiders.

Puppies are particularly social creatures, they need the company of other puppies when young. Suede and Cassanova cuddle during nap time.

Every pack has an Alpha figure. The dog looks to you, or should look to you, to be that leader. If your dog doesn't receive the proper training and guidance, he very well may replace you as Alpha. This would be a serious problem and is certainly a disservice to your dog.

You can tell a lot about a dog's personality by observing his body language. Timmy submits to his owner and gets an enjoyable tummy rub as his reward.

Eye contact is one way the Alpha wolf keeps order within his pack. You are Alpha so you must establish eye contact with your puppy. Obviously your puppy will have to look at you. Practice eye contact even if you need to hold his head for five to ten seconds at a time. You can give him a treat as a reward. Make sure your eye contact is gentle and not threatening. Later, if he has been naughty, it is permissible to give him a long, penetrating look. There are some older dogs that never learned eye contact as puppies and cannot accept eye contact. You should avoid eye contact with these dogs since they feel threatened and will retaliate as such.

BODY LANGUAGE

The play bow, when the forequarters are down and the hindquarters are elevated, is an invitation to play. Puppies play fight, which helps them learn the acceptable limits of biting. This is necessary for later in their lives. Nevertheless, an owner may be falsely reassured by the playful nature of his dog's aggression. Playful aggression toward another dog or human may be an indication of serious aggression in the future. Owners should never play fight or play tug-of-war with any dog that is inclined to be dominant.

Signs of submission are:
1. Avoids eye contact.
2. Active submission—the dog crouches down, ears back and the tail is lowered.
3. Passive submission—the dog rolls on his side with his hindlegs in the air and frequently urinates.

Signs of dominance are:
1. Makes eye contact.
2. Stands with ears up, tail up and the hair raised on his neck.

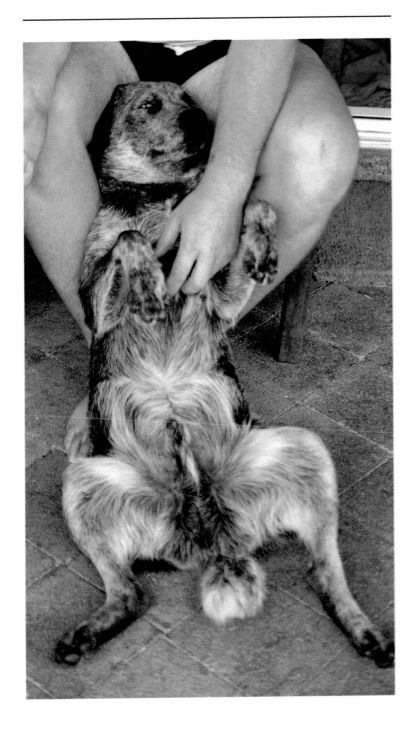

3. Shows dominance over another dog by standing at right angles over it.

Dominant dogs tend to behave in characteristic ways such as:

1. The dog may be unwilling to move from his place (i.e., reluctant to give up the sofa if the owner wants to sit there).
2. He may not part with toys or objects in his mouth and may show possessiveness with his food bowl.
3. He may not respond quickly to commands.
4. He may be disagreeable for grooming and dislikes to be petted.

Dogs are popular because of their sociable nature. Those that have contact with humans during the first 12 weeks of life regard them as a member of their own species—their pack. All dogs have the potential for both dominant and submissive behavior. Only through experience and training do they learn to whom it is appropriate to show which behavior. Not all dogs are concerned with dominance but owners need to be aware of that potential. It is wise for the owner to establish his dominance early on.

A human can express dominance or submission toward a dog in the following ways:

1. Meeting the dog's gaze signals dominance. Averting the gaze signals submission. If the dog growls or threatens, averting the gaze is the first avoiding action to take—it may prevent attack. It is important to establish eye contact in the puppy. The older dog that has not been exposed to eye contact may see it as a threat and will not be willing to submit.
2. Being taller than the dog signals dominance; being lower signals submission. This is why, when attempting to make friends with a strange dog or catch the runaway, one

A properly socialized Australian Cattle Dog will be able to get along with all the members of a household. PK and her friend enjoy each other's company.

should kneel down to his level. Some owners see their dogs become dominant when allowed on the furniture or on the bed. Then he is at the owner's level.

3. An owner can gain dominance by ignoring all the dog's social initiatives. The owner pays attention to the dog only when he obeys a command.

No dog should be allowed to achieve dominant status over any adult or child. Ways of preventing are as follows:

A child makes the perfect playmate for an energetic Australian Cattle Dog and caring for a dog teaches a child responsibility and respect for animals.

Your Australian Cattle Dog puppy must be taught to behave. The result will be a well-mannered and amiable companion.

A puppy should not be forced into a situation he finds frightening. Respect his feelings and allow him time to acclimate to the situation.

1. Handle the puppy gently, especially during the three- to four-month period.

2. Let the children and adults handfeed him and teach him to take food without lunging or grabbing.

3. Do not allow him to chase children or joggers.

4. Do not allow him to jump on people or mount their legs. Even females may be inclined to mount. It is not only a male habit.

5. Do not allow him to growl for any reason.

6. Don't participate in wrestling or tug-of-war games.

7. Don't physically punish puppies for aggressive behavior. Restrain him from repeating the infraction and teach an alternative behavior. Dogs should earn everything they receive from their owners. This would include sitting

to receive petting or treats, sitting before going out the door and sitting to receive the collar and leash. These types of exercises reinforce the owner's dominance.

Young children should never be left alone with a dog. It is important that children learn some basic obedience commands so they have some control over the dog. They will gain the respect of their dog.

FEAR

One of the most common problems dogs experience is being fearful. Some dogs are more afraid than others. On the lesser side, which is sometimes humorous to watch, dogs can be afraid of a strange object. They act silly when something is out of place in the house. We call his problem perceptive intelligence. He realizes the abnormal within his known environment. He does not react the same way in strange environments since he does not know what is normal.

Behavior and health problems can be passed down from generation to generation, so be sure to check your puppy's lineage very carefully.

On the more serious side is a fear of people. This can result in backing off, seeking his own space and saying "leave me alone" or it can result in an aggressive behavior that may lead to challenging the person. Respect that the dog wants to be left alone and give him time to come forward. If you approach the cornered dog, he may resort to snapping. If you leave him alone, he may decide to come forward, which should be rewarded with a treat.

Some dogs may initially be too fearful to take treats. In these cases it is helpful to make sure the dog hasn't eaten for about 24 hours. Being a little hungry encourages him to accept the treats, especially if they are of the "gourmet" variety.

Dogs can be afraid of numerous things, including loud noises and thunderstorms. Invariably the owner rewards (by comforting) the dog when it shows signs of fearfulness. When

your dog is frightened, direct his attention to something else and act happy. Don't dwell on his fright.

AGGRESSION

Some different types of aggression are: predatory, defensive, dominance, possessive, protective, fear induced, noise provoked, "rage" syndrome (unprovoked aggression), maternal and aggression directed toward other dogs. Aggression is the most common behavioral problem encountered. Protective breeds are expected to be more aggressive than others but with the proper upbringing they can make very dependable companions. You need to be able to read your dog.

It is important to remember that your Australian Cattle Dog wants to please you, and with patience he will learn what you have to teach him!

Many factors contribute to aggression including genetics and environment. An improper environment, which may include the living conditions, lack of social life, excessive punishment, being attacked or frightened by an aggressive dog, etc., can all influence a dog's behavior. Even spoiling him and giving too much praise may be detrimental. Isolation and the lack of human contact or exposure to frequent teasing by children or adults also can ruin a good dog.

Lack of direction, fear, or confusion lead to aggression in those dogs that are so inclined. Any obedience exercise, even the sit and down, can direct the dog and overcome fear and/or confusion. Every dog should learn these commands as a youngster, and there should be periodic reinforcement.

When a dog is showing signs of aggression, you should speak calmly (no screaming or hysterics) and firmly give a command that he understands, such as the sit. As soon as your dog obeys, you have assumed your dominant position. Aggression presents a problem because there may be danger to others. Sometimes it is an emotional issue. Owners may consciously or unconsciously

Training will be evident in your dog's good behavior. Ch. Kombinalong Super "K" is a fine example of a well-trained champion.

encourage their dog's aggression. Other owners show responsibility by accepting the problem and taking measures to keep it under control. The owner is responsible for his dog's actions, and it is not wise to take a chance on someone being bitten, especially a child. Euthanasia is the solution for some owners and in severe cases this may be the best choice. However, few dogs are that dangerous and very few are that much of a threat to their owners. If caution is exercised and professional help is gained early on, most cases can be controlled.

Some authorities recommend feeding a lower protein (less than 20 percent) diet. They believe this can aid in reducing aggression. If the dog loses weight, then vegetable oil can be added. Veterinarians and behaviorists are having some success with pharmacology. In many cases treatment is possible and can improve the situation.

If you have done everything according to "the book" regarding training and socializing and are still having a behavior problem, don't procrastinate. It is important that the problem gets attention before it is out of hand. It is estimated that 20 percent of a veterinarian's time may be devoted to dealing with problems before they become so intolerable that the dog is separated from its home and owner. If your veterinarian isn't able to help, he should refer you to a behaviorist.

PROBLEMS

Barking
This is a habit that shouldn't be encouraged. Some owners

Even though this Australian Cattle Dog looks relaxed and settled, there are all sorts of predicaments he can get into in the great outdoors. Always supervise him closely when outside.

desire their dog to bark so as to be a watchdog. Most dogs will bark when a stranger comes to the door.

The new puppy frequently barks or whines in the crate in his strange environment and the owner reinforces the puppy's bad behavior by going to him during the night. This is a no-no. Smack the top of the crate and say "quiet" in a loud, firm voice. The puppies don't like to hear the loud noise of the crate being banged. If the barking is sleep-interrupting, then the owner should take crate and pup to the bedroom for a few days until the puppy becomes adjusted to his new environment. Otherwise ignore the barking during the night.

Excessive barking can be an annoyance, but dogs also use their bark to "verbally" communicate. What is your Australian Cattle Dog trying to tell you?

Barking can be an inherited problem or a bad habit learned through the environment. It takes dedication to stop the barking. Attention should be paid to the cause of the barking. Does the dog seek attention, does he need to go out, is it feeding time, is it occurring when he is left alone, is it a protective bark, etc.? Overzealous barking is an inherited tendency. When barking presents a problem for you, try to stop it as soon as it begins.

There are electronic collars available that are supposed to curb barking. There are some disadvantages to to the collar. If the dog is barking out of excitement, punishment is not the appropriate treatment. Presumably there is the chance the collar could be activated by other stimuli and thereby punish the dog when it is not barking. Should you decide to use one, then you should seek help from a person with experience with that type of collar. Nevertheless the root of the problem needs to be investigated and corrected.

In extreme circumstances (usually when there is a problem with the neighbors), some people have resorted to having their dogs debarked. I caution you that the dog continues to bark but usually only a squeaking sound is heard. Frequently the

Does this look like the face of a mischief maker? This mellow guy enjoys relaxing in his owner's lawn chair!

vocal cords grow back. Probably the biggest concern is that the dog can be left with scar tissue which can narrow the opening to the trachea.

Jumping Up

A dog that jumps up is a happy dog. Nevertheless few guests appreciate dogs jumping on them. Clothes get footprinted and/or snagged.

Some trainers believe in allowing the puppy to jump up during his first few weeks. If you correct him too soon and at the wrong age you may intimidate him. Consequently he could be timid around humans later in his life. However, there will come a time, probably around four months of age, that he needs to know when it is okay to jump and when he is to show off good manners by sitting instead.

Some authorities never allow jumping. If you are irritated by your dog jumping up on you, then you should discourage it from the beginning. A larger breed of dog can cause harm to a senior citizen. Some are quite fragile. It may not take much to cause a topple that could break a hip.

How do you correct the problem? All family members need to participate in teaching the puppy to sit as soon as he starts to jump up. The sit must be practiced every time he starts to jump up. Don't forget to praise him for his good behavior. If an older dog has acquired the habit, grasp his paws and squeeze tightly. Give a firm "No." He'll soon catch on. Remember the entire family must take part. Each time you allow him to jump up you go back a step in training.

Biting

All puppies bite and try to chew on your fingers, toes, arms, etc. This is the time to teach them to be gentle and not bite hard. Put your fingers in your puppy's mouth and if he bites too hard then say "easy" and let him know he's hurting you. Squeal and act like you have been seriously hurt. If the puppy plays too rough and doesn't respond to your corrections, then he needs "Time Out" in his crate. You should be particularly careful with young children and puppies who still have their deciduous (baby) teeth. Those teeth are like needles and can leave little scars on youngsters.

Although some traits are inherited within a breed, every Australian Cattle Dog is an individual.

Biting in the more mature dog is something that should be prevented at all costs. Should it occur quickly let him know in no uncertain terms that biting will not be tolerated. When biting is directed toward another dog (dog fight), don't get in the middle of it. Some authorities recommend breaking up a fight by elevating the hind legs. This would only be possible if there was a person for each dog. Obviously it would be hard to fight with the hind legs off the ground. A dog bite is serious and should be given attention. Wash the bite with soap and water and contact your doctor. It is important to know the status of the offender's rabies vaccination.

Your dog must know who is boss. When biting occurs, you should seek professional help at once. On the other hand you must not let your dog intimidate you and be so afraid of a bite that you can't discipline him. Professional help through your veterinarian, dog trainer and/or behaviorist can give you guidance.

Digging

Bored dogs release their frustrations through mischievous behavior such as digging. Dogs shouldn't be left unattended outside, even if they are in a fenced-in yard. Usually the dog is sent to "jail" (the backyard) because the owner can't tolerate him in the house. The culprit feels socially deprived and needs to be included in the owner's life. The owner has neglected the dog's training. The dog has not developed into the companion we desire. If you are one of these owners, then perhaps it is possible for you to change. Give him another chance. Some owners object to their dog's unkempt coat and doggy odor. See that he is groomed on a regular schedule and look into some training classes.

Submissive Urination

This is not a housebreaking problem. It can occur in all breeds and may be more prevalent in some breeds. Usually it occurs in puppies but occasionally it occurs in older dogs and may be in response to physical praise. Try verbal praise or ignoring your dog until after he has had a chance to relieve himself. Scolding will only make the problem worse. Many dogs outgrow this problem.

Coprophagia

Also know as stool eating, sometimes occurs without a cause. It may begin with boredom and then becomes a habit that is hard to break. Your best remedy is to keep the puppy on a leash and keep the yard picked up. Then he won't have an opportunity to get in trouble. Your veterinarian can dispense a medication that is put on the dog's food that makes the stool taste bitter. Of course this will do little good if your dog cleans up after other dogs.

SUGGESTED READING

TS-214
Skin & Coat Care For Your Dog
Dr. Lowell Ackerman, DVM
432 pages, over 300 full-color photos

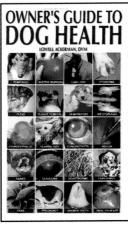

TS-249
Owner's Guide to Dog Health
Dr. Lowell Ackerman, DVM
224 pages, over 190 full-color photos

TS-252
Dog Behavior and Training
Edited by Dr. Lowell Ackerman,
DVM
292 pages, over 200 full-color photos

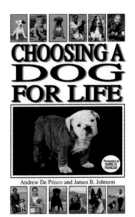

TS-257
Choosing A Dog for Life
Andres DePrisco and James
Johnson
384 pages, over 700 full-color photos

INDEX